A BOOK *of* HOURS

AND THE
PRACTICE
OF THE
GOLDEN RULE

SELECTIONS FROM THE CHRISTIAN SCRIPTURES,
THE PSALMS, AND OTHER SOURCES,
WITH ADDITIONAL NOTES

ART SCHULLER

FOREWORD — NICHOLAS PIEDISCALZI

ILLUSTRATIONS — GINNA BB GORDON

LUCKY VALLEY PRESS   CARMEL, CALIFORNIA

Copyright © 2014 by Art Schuller. All rights reserved.

Book design and typography by Lucky Valley Press
Cover illustration and design by Ginna BB Gordon
Photo of the author by Dinah Phillips

ISBN 978-0-9856655-3-1

Unless otherwise indicated, the Scripture quotations
contained herein are from the *New Revised Standard Version
Bible*, copyright 1989, by the Division of Christian Education
of the National Councils of the Churches of Christ in the
U.S.A. Used by permission. All rights reserved.

This book contains images and text protected under
International and Federal Copyright Laws and Treaties. No part
of this book may be reproduced or transmitted in any form or by
any means, electronic or mechanical, including photocopying,
recording, or by any information storage and retrieval system
without express written permission from the author.

Lucky Valley Press
Carmel, California
www.luckyvalleypress.com

Printed in the United States of America

Dedication

To
Albert Schweitzer,
Mahatma Gandhi,
and
Martin Luther King, Jr.,

and all the others like them,
both known and unknown,
for being doers of the word,
and not hearers only.

Table of Contents

DEDICATION	*vii*
APPRECIATION	*x*
FOREWORD	*xi*
INTRODUCTION	*xiii*

SUNDAY
Morning	*3*
Day	*7*
Evening	*11*
Night	*14*

MONDAY
Morning	*21*
Day	*27*
Evening	*33*
Night	*38*

TUESDAY
Morning	*45*
Day	*50*
Evening	*56*
Night	*60*

WEDNESDAY
Morning	*67*
Day	*72*
Evening	*79*
Night	*82*

THURSDAY
Morning	*89*
Day	*93*
Evening	*97*
Night	*100*

FRIDAY
Morning	*109*
Day	*113*
Evening	*116*
Night	*120*

SATURDAY
Morning	*129*
Day	*134*
Afternoon	*138*
Evening	*143*
Night	*153*

NOTES	*159*
ACKNOWLEDGEMENTS	*166*
ABOUT THE AUTHOR	*170*

Appreciation

Sandy Schuller, my friend, partner, and wife, whose love and thoughtfulness make both this book and my life better than I could ever imagine.

The Reverends David Dodson, David Grishaw-Jones, Wendy Howe, Nicholas Piediscalzi, and Cordelia Strandskov, who serve so that the gospel might be real in our lives.

Ginna and David Gordon of Lucky Valley Press, whose friendship, encouragement, creativity, and expertise made this book a reality.

Karen Armstrong, whose work champions the possibility of all of us loving our neighbors as ourselves.

Foreword

James Finley once said, "It would be so easy to be a mystic if only I didn't have to live my life."[1] Most of us feel that way. So did Art Schuller, as the demands of his life as a physician and the misadventures of our culture seemed to prevent him from living thoughtfully and compassionately with himself, his neighbors, and God, and left him with feelings of emptiness, estrangement, and fragmentation. He sought counsel from thoughtful people in his life, including his minister, David Grishaw-Jones, who wisely recommended that he develop a devotional practice and suggested that he begin by using Thomas Merton's *A Book of Hours*[2] as a guide. This he did. He made room in his busy life to cultivate, several times a day, a contemplative practice where, in the poetic lines of Walter Rauschenbusch (1861-1918), a founder of the Social Gospel Movement, he entered into the presence of God where

> Big things become small, and small things become great.
> The near becomes far, and the future is near.
> The lowly and despised is shot through with glory...
> God is the substance of all revolutions;
> When I am in Him, I am in the Kingdom of God
> And the Fatherland of my Soul.[3]

Like Rauschenbusch, Schuller began to discover that it is possible to live mindfully while engaged in our chaotic world, although it is a work that is always in progress. He learned that the mysticism that motivated Jesus' ministry did not call him out of the world and into the private realm where one dwells solely on solving personal spiritual problems; rather, it led Jesus into the world with his whole being, to work tirelessly for a justice based on compassion and inclusiveness. These lessons, along with Karen Armstrong's emphasis on cultivating a practice of "interpersonal" compassion,[4] turned Schuller to a contemplative study of Jesus' teachings about and practice of the golden rule. This pursuit inspired Schuller to engage in a number of projects, for example, participating with the group Communities Organized for Relational Power in Action (COPA),[5] to work persistently and patiently over an extended period of time to eventually persuade the Monterey County, California, Board of Supervisors to provide health care for the working poor - many of whom are immigrant farm laborers - living in their area.

Schuller also took seriously Armstrong's suggestion that her readers write their own devotional guides. This marvelous volume, a treasure chest of biblical readings, prayers, selected quotations from religious leaders, and Schuller's insightful comments, is his response. We are the fortunate beneficiaries of his "labor of love." I encourage you to join Schuller in his pilgrimage from "Galilee to Calvary, and back to Galilee," and experience a personal transformation that enables you to be sustained by a "peace that passeth all understanding"[6] as you live in our chaotic world and contribute to the building of a New Realm of Justice and Compassion.

Rev. Nicholas Piediscalzi, PhD
Professor Emeritus of Religion
Wright State University

Introduction

There must be a time of day when the man who
makes plans forgets his plans,
and acts as if he had no plans at all.

There must be a time of day when the man who has
to speak falls very silent.
And his mind forms no more propositions,
and he asks himself:
Did they have a meaning?

There must be a time
when the man of prayer goes to pray
as if it were the first time in his life
he had ever prayed,
when the man of resolutions puts his
resolutions aside
as if they had all been broken,
and he learns a different wisdom:

distinguishing the sun from the moon,
the stars from the darkness,
the sea from the dry land,
and the night sky from the shoulder of a hill.

                                                       Thomas Merton[1]

LUKE 6:31 "Do to others as you would have them do to you."

ROMANS 13:9 The commandments, "You shall not commit adultery; You shall not murder; You shall not steal; You shall not covet"; and any other commandment, are summed up in this word, "Love your neighbor as yourself."

Over there, where my neighbor or enemy is, is myself, most often unrecognized.

I notice how another person's actions toward me can affect my own and how mine can affect another's. If I mistreat one person, there is the likelihood of all creatures being mistreated. If I serve one person, there is the possibility of all creatures being served.

This book is intended to be a useful devotional tool in the real life practice of the golden rule. It is not about doctrine; rather it is about energizing the practice of loving God and my neighbor. Thank you for considering it. Let me begin by sharing with you some of how it came to be.

In the usual course of my day, there are frequent interruptions that distract me from living thoughtfully and compassionately in relationship with my family, friends, neighbors, and colleagues. I have loved this paraphrase of G. K. Chesterton's quote since the first time I heard it: "The Christian ideal has not been tried and found wanting; it has been found difficult and left untried."[2] Since I am committed to continuing to try, it seemed that several planned "interruptions" each day might help me recover myself in relationship with the people around me. Hence, this book of hours.

Books of hours have been used as devotionals by the laity since the middle ages. They provide some of the daily structured study, prayer, and reflection that can be found in monastic communities. The Forward and Introduction in Thomas Merton's *A Book of Hours* are helpful sources of information on the subject.[3]

My interest in books of hours began several years ago. My church's Senior Pastor, David Grishaw-Jones, suggested that I use Merton's book, which consists of selections from his writings, for reflection and contemplation through the day, for my devotional practice. I did and I found it to be very helpful.

In considering our behavior as human beings, where compassion seems to be most often expressed in the wish rather than the act, where we reflexively respond in ways that are hurtful to the well-being of others and ourselves, where being right is more important than effectively working together, I began to reflect more and more on the golden rule and Chesterton's quote. At the same time I became aware of the work of the religious historian Karen Armstrong, emphasizing the common element of a call to compassionate living in the world's faith traditions.[4] It seems that all of them were aware of the golden rule and were recommending it to their adherents! Imagine that! Armstrong advocated individuals creating their own devotional guides, using those materials that inspired and sustained them in compassionate practice. Thus encouraged, I began the project you are now reading. Almost as soon as I began, I wondered about working with others to assemble a "book of hours" about the practice of the golden rule that included other religious traditions. However, with effort, I restrained myself and continued working on *Jesus and the Practice of the Golden Rule.*

This book is shaped by who I am at this moment, which includes my history. I was raised in the Lutheran church. From my adolescence on, the lives of Albert Schweitzer,[5] Mahatma Gandhi,[6] and, later, Martin Luther King, Jr.,[7] profoundly affected me, including my decision to become a physician. My wife, Sandy, and I are active members of the Peace United Church of Christ in Santa Cruz, California.

My reading of scripture is sometimes metaphorical and sometimes historical. For example, I consider Jesus' walking on water and calling on Peter to do the same as an invitation to extraordinary service. (By the way, Peter and I have a lot in common, what with our many initial enthusiasms and subsequent, sometimes grave, missteps, and our dogged determination to continue as Jesus' disciples.) On the other hand, I trust that Jesus chose to die on the cross out of his love for his enemies as well as for his friends, including Judas. He could have gotten along with everyone, he could have fought back, he could have just left town. Instead, as John Howard Yoder discusses in *The Politics of Jesus*, he showed us the way of compassion and non-violence and continues to call us to follow him.[8]

The mystery we call God has given us the gifts of love and forgiveness and the opportunity to share them with each other, to give our lives to each other. When we do, extraordinary things happen. God wants me to love my neighbor as myself, even if my taxes go up. The God that I am grateful to for the opportunity of my life does not justify abusing or killing my neighbors, ever, or burning their holy books. God does not think that it is appropriate for people to go bankrupt to obtain necessary medical care or to die because they cannot afford it. God without ethics is an oxymoron.

In selecting the material for this book, I chose those excerpts from the Christian scriptures and the psalms that most clearly spoke to me of various aspects of the practice of the golden rule, recognizing that other readers, with the same purpose in mind, might have made other choices. From among the gospel excerpts, I selected those that seemed to me to create a flow in the narrative from Jesus' first calling his disciples to follow him to his final calling on them to feed his sheep. The introit, epistle, psalm, prayer, and benediction within each hour are intended to complement the gospel excerpt.

With regard to prayer, I do not think of it as a request for suspension of the laws of the physical universe, although at times I wish this were possible; rather it is an attempt to put into words my commitment to live out of my love of God and my neighbor.

The book is arranged in seven days, beginning with Sunday. Because a single structured time for devotion, for example, in the morning, was not sufficient to support me through the day, I adopted four hours: "Morning," "Day," "Evening," and "Night." Each hour is not a unit of time, that is, 60 minutes; rather it represents a variable period of time, from a few minutes to many minutes, given to interrupting the automaticity of the day with reflection and the possibility of spontaneity. On Saturday I added an "Afternoon" hour because of the extraordinary circumstances of Jesus' crucifixion. Also, since I inconsistently get to those things that I say I'll get to if I have the time, committing to four and five times a day gave me the opportunity to be responsible for managing my time, rather than having my time manage me.

The process of reading, reflecting, and selecting from the scriptures and other sources was a revealing one. It was not just that I learned more, although that happened as well. With the purpose of the project in mind, the more I read and re-read and re-re-read, my appreciation for what I was reading deepened in unexpected ways.

For example, the text from MATTHEW 9:16-17, "No one sews a piece of un-shrunk cloth on an old cloak, for the patch pulls away from the cloak, and a worse tear is made. Neither is new wine put into old wineskins; otherwise, the skins burst, and the wine is spilled, and the skins are destroyed; but new wine is put into fresh wineskins, and so both are preserved."

In the past, I had read that passage many times and moved on. As I read, re-read, re-re-read, and reflected on it during this project, I remembered someone telling me about Albert Einstein's description of the insight which led to his formulation of the theory of relativity. Einstein is supposed to have said that at that moment he was out of his mind, that is, he was thinking "outside the box" of Newtonian physics. I was also told that one cannot derive the theory of relativity from Newtonian physics. The theory of relativity is not an extension of Newtonian physics. It is a brand new physics.

About the golden rule, I saw that it was no longer about always "being nice," or even about always "being really nice." In addition, it was definitely not about being passive. Rather it was an invitation to an extremely unreasonable, intrusive, and disquieting way of being in the world, redefining who I am and who my neighbor is and what I do to, for, and with my neighbor. I hope that you, too, find this book disquieting in a way that serves you in participating ever more fully and compassionately with the people in your life.

I think you will have to discover for yourself how to best use *Jesus and the Practice of the Golden Rule*. What follow are suggestions for your consideration. Begin by reading the entire book to acquaint yourself with the content and flow. Then give yourself four times a day (five times on Saturday), in a setting that works for you. While you may choose to practice the hours alone, you might also consider observing them with a partner or a group.

James Finley says that since each hour is an occasion for quiet reflection and listening, rather than reading for information, or even inspiration, read the excerpts in their entirety, or in part, whichever serves you best. Give yourself the opportunity to listen for the "stop-dead-in-your-track one-liners" and consider those.[9] You can also use the method of *lectiodivina*, or sacred study, to give more structure to your practice. Deignan,[10] Armstrong.[11] It includes reading the text; meditating on the text, that is, keeping the text in mind by repetition or memorization; praying on the text and those concerns that the text raises for you; and contemplation, that is, using the Quiet time to sit "motionless in silence, attentive and awake to the abyss-like nature of each breath," Finley,[12] and allowing yourself to be moved "beyond all words, images, and concepts toward a quiet abiding in wordless silence." Deignan[13] If you find yourself distracted, as everyone does at some time, gently bring your attention back to your reading, meditating, praying, or contemplating. And listen anew.

And with the admonition in mind to remove the log from my own eye before going after the speck in my neighbor's eye, wherever the text says, "angry crowd," "blind man," "demoniac," "Gentiles," "goats," "high priest," "James and John, the sons of Zebedee," "Jews," "Judas," "lawyer," "leper," "Levite," "lost sheep," "Peter," "priest," "Pharisee," "rich man," "scribe," "sinner," "tax collector," etc., I put in my own name. I suggest that you try putting in yours.

Also, please remember, this is a book for both of us, you and me. That is, we are both, we are all, works in progress and shall be for the foreseeable future. The gospel song sings for all of us, "Keep your hand on the plow, hold on."

When I shared a draft of *Jesus and the Practice of the Golden Rule* with my church's Associate Pastor, Cordelia Strandskov, she suggested that I include the use of music as an option during each hour. Since music is a very important part of my life, I was surprised that I had not considered it, but grateful that she had. I am both moved and quieted by Gregorian chant and found it fitting for me when I tried it during the Quiet time, as well as during the entire hour. I have listed several chant recordings in the Notes section, under Discography. Of course, you can use any music that serves you. For those that might be interested, I have also included a reference on how we are affected by music in the Notes section, under Additional Suggested Reading.

The gospel and epistle selections are from the *New Revised Standard Version Bible* for the more familiar, contemporary language usage. My age and up-bringing dictated that the psalm selections are from the *King James Version* for the beauty and elegance of the language and poetry.

All the verses are noted at the beginning of each scripture selection. My insertions are marked by square brackets and omissions by triple dots. The references for the numbered passages are found in the Notes section, under the corresponding chapter, that is, "Introduction," "Sunday," "Monday," etc. I thought it appropriate to repeat some of the excerpts.

My notes are printed in italics.

So then, let us walk with Jesus from Galilee to Calvary, and back to Galilee, this week and in the weeks to come. And let us ask him to live through us, guiding us in the days given to us, to be his heart and hands in the world.

"I hope these few words will be of some help. I send you all my blessings and I join you in your happiness. I am glad to have had some small part in God's work for you."

Thomas Merton[14]

Amen.

Art Schuller
Carmel Valley, California
June, 2014

Sunday

Sunday

Morning

Introit

Consider the mystery of creation with wonder, the gift of creation with gratitude, and your neighbor as yourself.

Gospel

MATTHEW 1:1-16 An account of the genealogy of Jesus the Messiah, the son of David, the son of Abraham. Abraham was the father of Isaac, and Isaac the father of Jacob, and Jacob the father of Judah and his brothers, and Judah the father of Perez and Zerah by Tamar, and Perez the father of Hezron, and Hezron the father of Aram, and Aram the father of Aminadab, and Aminadab the father of Nahshon, and Nahshon the father of Salmon, and Salmon the father of Boaz by Rahab, and Boaz the father of Obed by Ruth, and Obed the father of Jesse, and Jesse the father of King David. And David was the father of Solomon by the wife of Uriah, and Solomon the father of Rehoboam, and Rehoboam the father of Abijah, and Abijah the father of Asaph, and Asaph the father of Jehoshaphat, and Jehoshaphat the father of Joram, and Joram the father of Uzziah, and Uzziah the father of Jotham, and Jotham the father of Ahaz, and Ahaz the father of Hezekiah, and Hezekiah the father of Manasseh, and Manasseh the father of Amos, and Amos the father of Josiah, and Josiah the father of Jechoniah and his brothers, at the time of the deportation to Babylon. And after the deportation to Babylon: Jechoniah was the father of Salathiel, and Salathiel the father of Zerubbabel, and Zerubbabel the father of Abiud, and Abiud the father of Eliakim, and Eliakim the father of Azor, and Azor the father of Zadok, and Zadok the father of Achim, and Achim the father of Eliud, and Eliud the father of Eleazar, and Eleazar the father of Matthan, and Matthan the father of Jacob, and Jacob the father of Joseph the husband of Mary, of whom Jesus was born, who is called the Messiah.

Gail Godwin used this gospel reading for an Advent Sunday sermon: that God does not necessarily select the noblest or most deserving person to carry out divine purposes.[1]

Consider that it will take all of us, each and every one of us, the common, the uncommon, the good, the bad, the known, the unknown, the likely, the unlikely, the pretty, the plain, all of us, each and every one of us, to be the change we want to see.[2]

Epistle

ROMANS 7:15 I do not understand my own actions. For I do not do what I want, but I do the very thing I hate.

ROMANS 8:5-6, 26-28 For those who live according to the flesh, set their minds on the things of the flesh, but those who live according to the Spirit set their minds on the things of the Spirit. To set the mind on the flesh is death, but to set the mind on the Spirit is life and peace. Likewise the Spirit helps us in our weakness; for we do not know how to pray as we ought, but that very Spirit intercedes with sighs too deep for words. And God, who searches the heart, knows what is the mind of the Spirit, because the Spirit intercedes for the saints according to the will of God.

Psalm

PSALM 1:1-3 Blessed is the man that walketh not in the counsel of the ungodly, nor standeth in the way of sinners, nor sitteth in the seat of the scornful. But his delight is in the law of the LORD; and in his law doth he meditate day and night. And he shall be like a tree planted by the rivers of water, that bringeth forth his fruit in his season; his leaf also shall not wither; and whatsoever he doeth shall prosper.

Quiet

Prayer

Our Father who art in Heaven, hallowed be Thy name. Thy Kingdom come. Thy will be done on earth, as it is in Heaven. Give us this day our daily bread. And forgive us our debts, as we forgive our debtors. And lead us not into temptation, but deliver us from evil. For Thine is the Kingdom, and the power and the glory for ever. Amen.

Benediction

ROMANS 11:33 O the depth of the riches and wisdom and knowledge of God! How unsearchable are his judgments and how inscrutable his ways!

Sunday

Day

Introit

What will give you your life? What will you give your life for?

Gospel

LUKE 5:1-11 Once while Jesus was standing beside the lake of Gennesaret, and the crowd was pressing in on him to hear the word of God, he saw two boats there at the shore of the lake; the fishermen had gone out of them and were washing their nets. He got into one of the boats, the one belonging to Simon, and asked him to put out a little way from the shore. Then he sat down and taught the crowds from the boat. When he had finished speaking, he said to Simon, "Put out into the deep water and let down your nets for a catch." Simon answered, "Master, we have worked all night long but have caught nothing. Yet if you say so, I will let down the nets." When they had done this, they caught so many fish that their nets were beginning to break. So they signaled their partners in the other boat to come and help them. And they came and filled both boats, so that they began to sink. But when Simon

Peter saw it, he fell down at Jesus' knees, saying, "Go away from me, Lord, for I am a sinful man!" For he and all who were with him were amazed at the catch of fish that they had taken; and so also were James and John, sons of Zebedee, who were partners with Simon. Then Jesus said to Simon, "Do not be afraid; from now on you will be catching people." When they had brought their boats to shore, they left everything and followed him.

Albert Schweitzer described Jesus' calling of the disciples and us as an urgent invitation to an ethical vocation:

It is as though Jesus were speaking to all centuries to come: First see to it, I beg you, that man does not perish. Go after him as I went after him and find him where he is, where others have not found him, in filth, in neglect, in indignity. Live with him and help him to become a man again.

Jesus has welded religion and humanity so closely together that religion no longer exists as a separate entity; without true humanity, there is no religion.[3]

Epistle

ROMANS 12:2-8 Do not be conformed to this world, but be transformed by the renewing of your minds, so that you may discern what is the will of God - what is good and acceptable and perfect. For by the grace given to me I say to everyone among you not to think of yourself more highly than you ought to think, but think with sober judgment, each according to the measure of faith that God has assigned. For as in one body we have many members, and not all the members have the same function, so we, who are many, are one body in Christ, and individually we are members one of another. We have gifts that differ according to the grace given to us: prophecy, in proportion to faith; ministry, in ministering; the teacher, in teaching; the exhorter, in exhortation; the giver, in generosity; the leader, in diligence; the compassionate, in cheerfulness.

Psalm

PSALM 86:11-13, 15 Teach me thy way, O LORD; I will walk in thy truth: unite my heart to [regard thy name with wonder.] I will praise thee, O Lord my God, with all my heart: and I will glorify thy name for evermore. For great is thy mercy toward me: and thou hast delivered my soul from the lowest hell. ...thou, O Lord, art a God full of compassion, and gracious, longsuffering, and plenteous in mercy and truth.

Quiet

Prayer

O Lord, I offer myself and all that I have or am, to thee. Do with me, my God, whatever thou pleasest.

William Gahan[4]

Benediction

ROMANS 12:2 Do not be conformed to this world, but be transformed by the renewing of your minds, so that you may discern what is the will of God - what is good and acceptable and perfect.

Sunday

Evening

Introit

MATTHEW 9:16-17 "No one sews a piece of un-shrunk cloth on an old cloak, for the patch pulls away from the cloak, and a worse tear is made. Neither is new wine put into old wineskins; otherwise, the skins burst, and the wine is spilled, and the skins are destroyed; but new wine is put into fresh wineskins, and so both are preserved."

Listen, not again, but for the first time. These are new sayings. These are unreasonable sayings. You have not heard anything like them before.

Gospel

MATTHEW 5:1-11, 14-16 When Jesus saw the crowds, he went up the mountain; and after he sat down, his disciples came to him. Then Jesus began to speak, and taught them, saying: "Blessed are the poor in spirit, for theirs is the kingdom of heaven. Blessed are those who mourn, for they will be comforted. Blessed are the meek, for they will inherit the earth. Blessed are those who hunger and thirst for righteousness, for they will be filled. Blessed are the merciful, for they will receive mercy. Blessed are the pure in heart, for they will see God. Blessed are the peacemakers, for they will be called children of God. Blessed are those who are persecuted for righteousness' sake, for theirs is the kingdom of heaven. Blessed are you when people revile you and persecute you and utter all kinds of evil against you falsely on my account.

"You are the light of the world. A city built on a hill cannot be hid. No one after lighting a lamp puts it under the bushel basket, but on the lamp stand, and it gives light to all in the house. In the same way, let your light shine before others, so that they may see your good works and give glory to your Father in heaven."

Epistle

ROMANS 13:8-10 Owe no one anything, except to love one another; for the one who loves another has fulfilled the law. The commandments, "You shall not commit adultery; You shall not murder; You shall not steal; You shall not covet;" and any other commandment, are summed up in this word, "Love your neighbor as yourself." Love does no wrong to a neighbor; therefore, love is the fulfilling of the law.

Psalm

PSALM 119:104-5, 108 Through thy precepts I get understanding… Thy word is a lamp unto my feet, and a light unto my path. Accept, I beseech thee, the freewill offerings of my mouth, O LORD, and teach me thy judgments.

Quiet

Prayer

Father, help me to love my neighbor as myself, and when I do not, help me to clean up the mess. Amen.

Benediction

While we are told that they are already blessed, if you love the poor in spirit, those who mourn, the meek, those who hunger and thirst for righteousness, the merciful, the pure in heart, the peacemakers, those who are persecuted for righteousness' sake, and those who are reviled and persecuted and against whom all kinds of evil is uttered falsely, and do something about it, they will be doubly blessed.

Sunday

Night

Introit

Pray for grace to see and hear. Then look and listen.

Gospel

MATTHEW 5:21-24, 38-48 "You have heard that it was said to those of ancient times, 'You shall not murder;' and 'whoever murders shall be liable to judgment.' But I say to you that if you are angry with a brother or sister, you will be liable to judgment; and if you insult a brother or sister, you will be liable to the council; and if you say, 'You fool,' you will be liable to the hell of fire."

Even worse than being liable to judgment, or to the council, or to the hell of fire, with your anger and insults you will have sacrificed your capacity to love your brother or sister for the sake of your self-righteousness.

"So when you are offering your gift at the altar, if you remember that your brother or sister has something against you, leave your gift there before the altar and go; first be reconciled to your brother or sister, and then come and offer your gift.

"You have heard that it was said, 'An eye for an eye and a tooth for a tooth.' But I say to you, Do not resist an evildoer. But if anyone strikes you on the right cheek, turn the other also; and if anyone wants to sue you and take your coat, give your cloak as well; and if anyone forces you to go one mile, go also the second mile. Give to everyone who begs from you, and do not refuse anyone who wants to borrow from you.

"You have heard that it was said, 'You shall love your neighbor and hate your enemy.' But I say to you, Love your enemies and pray for those who persecute you, so that you may be children of your Father in heaven; for he makes his sun rise on the evil and on the good, and sends rain on the righteous and on the unrighteous. For if you love those who love you, what reward do you have? Do not even the tax collectors do the same? And if you greet only your brothers and sisters, what more are you doing than others? Do not even the Gentiles do the same? Be perfect, therefore, as your heavenly Father is perfect."

LUKE 6:31-38 "Do to others as you would have them do to you. If you love those who love you, what credit is that to you? For even sinners love those who love them. If you do good to those who do good to you, what credit is that to you? For even sinners do the same. If you lend to those from whom you hope to receive, what credit is that to you? Even sinners lend to sinners, to receive as much again. But love your enemies, do good, and lend, expecting nothing in return. Your reward will be great, and you will be children of the Most High; for he is kind to the ungrateful and the wicked. Be merciful, just as your Father is merciful. Do not judge, and you will not be judged; do not condemn, and you will not be condemned. Forgive, and you will be forgiven; give, and it will be given to you. A good measure, pressed down, shaken together, running over, will be put into your lap; for the measure you give will be the measure you get back."

Epistle

ROMANS 12:9-21 Let love be genuine; hate what is evil, hold fast to what is good; love one another with mutual affection; outdo one another in showing honor. Do not lag in zeal, be ardent in spirit, serve the Lord. Rejoice in hope, be patient in suffering, persevere in prayer. Contribute to the needs of the saints; extend hospitality to strangers. Bless those who persecute you; bless and do not curse them. Rejoice with those who rejoice, weep with those who weep. Live in harmony with one another; do not be haughty, but associate with the lowly; do not claim to be wiser than you are. Do not repay anyone evil for evil, but take thought for what is noble in the sight of all. If it is possible, so far as it depends on you, live peaceably with all. Beloved, never avenge yourselves, but leave room for the wrath of God; for it is written, "Vengeance is mine, I will repay, says the Lord." No, "if your enemies are hungry, feed them; if they are thirsty, give them something to drink; for by doing this you will heap burning coals on their heads." Do not be overcome by evil, but overcome evil with good.

Psalm

PSALM 107:1, 8-9 O give thanks unto the LORD, for he is good: for his mercy endureth for ever. Oh that men would praise the LORD for his goodness, and for his wonderful works to the children of men! For he satisfieth the longing soul, and filleth the hungry soul with goodness.

And for his wise counsel, give thanks unto the LORD.

Quiet

Prayer

Eternal Father, source of life and light, whose love extends to all people, all creatures, all things: Grant us that reverence for life which becomes those who believe in you; lest we despise it, degrade it, or come callously to destroy it. Rather let us save it, secure it, and sanctify it, after the example of your Son, Jesus Christ our Lord.

Robert Runcie[5]

Benediction

Night is at hand. Praise then darkness and Creation unfinished.
Ursula K. Le Guin[6]

Monday

Monday

Morning

Introit

The lovers of God have no religion but God alone.

Rumi[1]

Gospel

MATTHEW 6:1-18 "Beware of practicing your piety before others in order to be seen by them; for then you have no reward from your Father in heaven. So whenever you give alms, do not sound a trumpet before you, as the hypocrites do in the synagogues and in the streets, so that they may be praised by others. Truly I tell you, they have received their reward. But when you give alms, do not let your left hand know what your right hand is doing, so that your alms may be done in secret; and your Father who sees in secret will reward you. And whenever you pray, do not be like the hypocrites; for they love to stand and pray in the synagogues and at the street corners, so that they may be seen by others. Truly I tell you, they have received their reward. But whenever you pray, go into your room and shut the door and pray to your Father who is in secret; and your Father who sees in secret will reward you. When you are praying, do not heap up empty phrases as the Gentiles do; for they think that they will be heard because of their many words. Do not be like them, for your Father knows what you need before you ask him.

"Pray then in this way: Our Father in heaven, hallowed be your name. Your kingdom come. Your will be done, on earth as it is in heaven. Give us this day our daily bread. And forgive us our debts, as we also have forgiven our debtors. And do not bring us to the time of trial, but rescue us from the evil one. For if you forgive others their trespasses, your heavenly Father will also forgive you; but if you do not forgive others, neither will your Father forgive your trespasses."

Consider that if you do not forgive others, your life will be consumed by your resentments.

"And whenever you fast, do not look dismal, like the hypocrites, for they disfigure their faces so as to show others that they are fasting. Truly I tell you, they have received their reward. But when you fast, put oil on your head and wash your face, so that your fasting may be seen not by others but by your Father who is in secret; and your Father who sees in secret will reward you."

MATTHEW 7:7-12 "Ask, and it will be given you; search, and you will find; knock, and the door will be opened for you. For everyone who asks receives, and everyone who searches finds, and for everyone who knocks, the door will be opened. Is there anyone among you who, if your child asks for bread, will give a stone?

Or if the child asks for a fish, will give a snake? If you then, who are evil, know how to give good gifts to your children, how much more will your Father in heaven give good things to those who ask him!

"In everything do to others as you would have them do to you; for this is the law and the prophets."

Epistle

ROMANS 14:1-6, 10, 13, 18-20 Welcome those who are weak in the faith, but not for the purpose of quarreling over opinions. For example, some believe in eating anything, while the weak eat only vegetables. Those who eat must not despise those who abstain, and those who abstain must not pass judgment on those who eat; for God has welcomed them all. Who are you to pass judgment on the servants of another? It is before their own Lord that they stand or fall. And they will be upheld, for the Lord is able to make them stand. Some judge one day to be better than another, while others judge all days to be alike. Let all be fully convinced in their own minds. Those who observe the day, observe it in honor of the Lord. Also those who eat, eat in honor of the Lord, since they give thanks to God; while those who abstain, abstain in honor of the Lord and give thanks to God.

Why do you pass judgment on your brother or sister? Or you, why do you despise your brother or sister? Let us therefore no longer pass judgment on one another, but resolve instead never to put a stumbling block or hindrance in the way of another. The one who thus serves Christ is acceptable to God and has human approval. Let us then pursue what makes for peace and for mutual up-building. Do not, for the sake of food, destroy the work of God.

And do not, for the sake of any other custom, ritual, or tradition, destroy the work of God.

Psalm

PSALM 122:1-4, 6-9 I was glad when they said unto me, Let us go into the house of the LORD. Our feet shall stand within thy gates, O Jerusalem. Jerusalem is built as a city that is compact together: Whither the tribes go up, the tribes of the LORD, unto the testimony of Israel, to give thanks unto the name of the LORD. Pray for the peace of Jerusalem: they shall prosper that love thee. Peace be within thy walls, and prosperity within thy palaces. For my brethren and companions' sakes, I will now say, Peace be within thee. Because of the house of the LORD our God I will seek thy good.

Quiet

Prayer

Eternal Spirit,
Life-Giver, Pain-Bearer, Love-Maker,
Source of all that is and that shall be,
Father and Mother of us all,
Loving God, in whom is heaven:

The Hallowing of your Name
   echo through the universe!
The Way of your Justice
   be followed by the peoples of the world!
Your Heavenly Will
   be done by all created beings!
Your Commonwealth of Peace and Freedom
   sustain our hope and come on earth.

With the bread we need for today,
   feed us.
In the hurts we absorb from one another,
   forgive us.
In times of temptation and test,
   strengthen us.
From trials too great to endure,
   spare us.
From the grip of all that is evil,
   free us.

For you reign in the glory
of the power that is love,
now and for ever. Amen.

                                            Jim Cotter[2]

Benediction

I CORINTHIANS 14:20 Brothers and sisters, do not be children in your thinking; rather, be infants in evil, but in thinking be adults.

II CORINTHIANS 13:11 Put things in order, listen to my appeal, agree with one another, live in peace; and the God of love and peace will be with you.

Monday

Day

Introit

MATTHEW 6:33 "But strive first for the kingdom of God and his righteousness, and all these things will be given to you as well."

Gospel

MATTHEW 6:19-21, 24-33 "Do not store up for yourselves treasures on earth, where moth and rust consume and where thieves break in and steal; but store up for yourselves treasures in heaven, where neither moth nor rust consumes and where thieves do not break in and steal. For where your treasure is, there your heart will be also. No one can serve two masters; for a slave will either hate the one and love the other, or be devoted to the one and despise the other. You cannot serve God and wealth.

"Therefore I tell you, do not worry about your life, what you will eat or what you will drink, or about your body, what you will wear. Is not life more than food, and the body more than clothing? Look at the birds of the air; they neither sow nor reap nor gather into barns, and yet your heavenly Father feeds them. Are you not of more value than they? And can any of you by worrying add a single hour to your span of life? And why do you worry about clothing? Consider the lilies of the field, how they grow; they neither toil nor spin, yet I tell you, even Solomon in all his glory was not clothed like one of these. But if God so clothes the grass of the field, which is alive today and tomorrow is thrown into the oven, will he not much more clothe you - you of little faith? Therefore do not worry, saying, 'What will we eat?' or 'What will we drink?' or 'What will we wear?' For it is the Gentiles who strive for all these things; and indeed your heavenly Father knows that you need all these things. But strive first for the kingdom of God and his righteousness, and all these things will be given to you as well."

Epistle

I CORINTHIANS 11:23-25 …the Lord Jesus on the night when he was betrayed took a loaf of bread, and when he had given thanks, he broke it and said, "This is my body that is for you. Do this in remembrance of me." In the same way he took the cup also, after supper, saying, "This cup is the new covenant in my blood. Do this, as often as you drink it, in remembrance of me."

Do this in remembrance of him. Indeed, do everything that you do in remembrance of him.

Psalm

PSALM 90:1-2, 4-6, 10, 12, 16-17 LORD, thou hast been our dwelling place in all generations. Before the mountains were brought forth, or ever thou hadst formed the earth and the world, even from everlasting to everlasting, thou art God. For a thousand years in thy sight are but as yesterday when it is past, and as a watch in the night. Thou carriest them away as with a flood; they are as a sleep: in the morning they are like grass which groweth up. In the morning it flourisheth, and groweth up; in the evening it is cut down, and withereth. The days of our years are threescore years and ten; and if by reason of strength they be fourscore years, yet is their strength labour and sorrow; for it is soon cut off, and we fly away. So teach us to number our days, that we may apply our hearts unto wisdom. Let thy work appear unto thy servants, and thy glory unto their children. And let the beauty of the LORD our God be upon us: and establish thou the work of our hands upon us; yea, the work of our hands establish thou it.

Quiet

Prayer

Thou whom I speak of,
But who art beyond my speaking,
Thou who hast given me the gift of the birds of the air
And myself,
May I be grateful for whatever befalls me
And work every circumstance for the good of all around me.

Whatever there is to see of Thee
May others see in me
And may I see in them.

As Thou dost hold me in Thy love,
May I hold others in mine
And may I serve them.

May all that I am and do honor Thee.

Help me defeat my groundless worries
For both the birds of the air and I
Are under Thy hand
And abide in Thee.

Benediction

MATTHEW 6:33 "But strive first for the kingdom of God and his righteousness, and all these things will be given to you as well."

Monday

Evening

Introit

Kyrie Eleison, Christe Eleison, Kyrie Eleison
Kyrie Eleison, Christe Eleison, Kyrie Eleison
Kyrie Eleison, Christe Eleison, Kyrie Eleison

Lord have mercy, Christ have mercy, Lord have mercy
Lord have mercy, Christ have mercy, Lord have mercy
Lord have mercy, Christ have mercy, Lord have mercy

Gospel

MATTHEW 7:1-5 "Do not judge, so that you may not be judged. For with the judgment you make you will be judged, and the measure you give will be the measure you get. Why do you see the speck in your neighbor's eye, but do not notice the log in your own eye? Or how can you say to your neighbor, 'Let me take the speck out of your eye,' while the log is in your own eye? You hypocrite, first take the log out of your own eye, and then you will see clearly to take the speck out of your neighbor's eye."

JOHN 8:2-11 Early in the morning he came again to the temple. All the people came to him and he sat down and began to teach them. The scribes and the Pharisees brought a woman who had been caught in adultery; and making her stand before all of them, they said to him, "Teacher, this woman was caught in the very act of committing adultery. Now in the law Moses commanded us to stone such women. Now what do you say?" They said this to test him, so that they might have some charge to bring against him. Jesus bent down and wrote with his finger on the ground. When they kept on questioning him, he straightened up and said to them, "Let anyone among you who is without sin be the first to throw a stone at her." And once again he bent down and wrote on the ground. When they heard it, they went away, one by one, beginning with the elders; and Jesus was left alone with the woman standing before him. Jesus straightened up and said to her, "Woman, where are they? Has no one condemned you?" She said, "No one, sir." And Jesus said, "Neither do I condemn you. Go your way, and from now on do not sin again.

Epistle

I CORINTHIANS 13:1-13 If I speak in the tongues of mortals and of angels, but do not have love, I am a noisy gong or a clanging cymbal. And if I have prophetic powers, and understand all mysteries and all knowledge, and if I have all faith, so as to remove mountains, but do not have love, I am nothing. If I give away all my possessions, and if I hand over my body so that I may boast, but do not have love, I gain nothing. Love is patient; love is kind; love is not envious or boastful or arrogant or rude. It does not insist on its own way; it is not irritable or resentful; it does not rejoice in wrongdoing, but rejoices in the truth. It bears all things, believes all things, hopes all things, endures all things. Love never ends. But as for prophecies, they will come to an end; as for tongues, they will cease; as for knowledge, it will come to an end. For we know only in part, and we prophesy only in part; but when the complete comes, the partial will come to an end. When I was a child, I spoke like a child, I thought like a child, I reasoned like a child; when I became an adult, I put an end to childish ways. For now we see in a mirror, dimly, but then we will see face to face. Now I know only in part; then I will know fully, even as I have been fully known. And now faith, hope, and love abide, these three; and the greatest of these is love.

Psalm

PSALM 103:1-6, 8, 10-18, 21-22 Bless the LORD, O my soul: and all that is within me, bless his holy name. Bless the LORD, O my soul, and forget not all his benefits: Who forgiveth all thine iniquities; who healeth all thy diseases. Who redeemeth thy life from destruction; who crowneth thee with lovingkindness and tender mercies; Who satisfieth thy mouth with good things; so that thy youth is renewed like the eagle's. The LORD executeth righteousness and judgment for all that are oppressed. The LORD is merciful and gracious, slow to anger, and plenteous in mercy. He hath not dealt with us after our sins; nor rewarded us according to our iniquities. For as the heaven is high above the earth, so great is his mercy toward them that [regard him with wonder.] As far as the east is from the west, so far hath he removed our transgressions from us. Like as a father pitieth his children, so the LORD pitieth [us.] For he knoweth our frame; he remembereth that we are dust. As for man, his days are as grass: as a flower of the field, so he flourisheth. For the wind passeth over it, and it is gone; and the place thereof shall know it no more. But the mercy of the LORD is from everlasting to everlasting upon them that [regard him with wonder,] and his righteousness unto our children's children; To such as keep his covenant, and to those who remember his commandments to do them. Bless ye the LORD, all ye his hosts; ye ministers of his, that do his pleasure. Bless the LORD, all his works in all places of his dominion: bless the LORD, O my soul.

Quiet

Prayer

O God, who hast bound us together in this bundle of life, give us grace to understand how our lives depend on the courage, the industry, the honesty, and the integrity of our fellow-men; that we may be mindful of their needs, grateful for their faithfulness, and faithful in our responsibilities to them; through Jesus Christ our Lord. Amen.

Reinhold Niebuhr[4]

Benediction

Pray that your life is shaped by love, and prepare to bear, believe, hope, and endure all things. And consider that bearing and enduring refer to patience, not to putting up with; and that believing and hoping refer to faith and trust, not to wishful thinking.

Monday

Night

Introit

Gratitude and generosity. You got the opportunity for your life for nothing. You got the opportunity to share it, also for nothing. Therefore, when asked, be generous in giving away what you got for nothing.

Gospel

LUKE 5:12-13 Once, when he was in one of the cities, there was a man covered with leprosy. When he saw Jesus, he bowed with his face to the ground and begged him, "Lord, if you choose, you can make me clean." Then Jesus stretched out his hand, touched him, and said, "I do choose. Be made clean." Immediately the leprosy left him.

Who is asking you to choose to do what you can?

LUKE 17:11-19 On the way to Jerusalem Jesus was going through the region between Samaria and Galilee. As he entered a village, ten lepers approached him. Keeping their distance, they called out, saying, "Jesus, Master, have mercy on us!" When he saw them, he said to them, "Go and show yourselves to the priests." And as they went, they were made clean. Then one of them, when he saw that he was healed, turned back, praising God with a loud voice. He prostrated himself at Jesus' feet and thanked him. And he was a Samaritan. Then Jesus asked, "Were not ten made clean? But the other nine, where are they? Was none of them found to return and give praise to God except this foreigner?" Then he said to him, "Get up and go on your way; your faith has made you well."

To whom and for what have you not expressed your gratitude?

Epistle

II THESSALONIANS 3:13 Brothers and sisters, do not be weary in doing what is right.

EPHESIANS 6:7 Render service with enthusiasm, as to the Lord...

Psalm

PSALM 143:8, 10 Cause me to hear thy loving kindness in the morning; for in thee do I trust: cause me to know the way wherein I should walk; for I lift up my soul unto thee. Teach me to do thy will; for thou art my God: thy spirit is good; lead me into the land of uprightness.

Quiet

Prayer

Thou art never weary, O Lord, of doing us good. Let us never weary of doing thee service. But, as thou hast pleasure in the prosperity of thy servants, so let us take pleasure in the service of our Lord, and abound in thy work and in thy love and praise, evermore. O fill up all that is wanting, reform whatever is amiss in us, perfect the thing that concerneth us. Let the witness of thy pardoning love ever abide in all our hearts.

John Wesley[6]

Benediction

Even though you know that you cannot possibly do all the good that needs to be done to remedy all the ills that need to be remedied and heal all the wounds that need to be healed, there may be times when you think and feel that is precisely what you must do. Consider that even Jesus did not take that on. He asked others to help him.

Your burden is not infinite nor everlasting and you are not alone. Ask and be willing to receive. And now rest.

Tuesday

Tuesday

Morning

Introit

O Lord, thank you for the gift of this night's rest. I offer you all that I do today. Amen.

Gospel

LUKE 5:17-25 One day, while he was teaching, Pharisees and teachers of the law were sitting near by (they had come from every village of Galilee and Judea and from Jerusalem); and the power of the Lord was with him to heal. Just then some men came, carrying a paralyzed man on a bed. They were trying to bring him in and lay him before Jesus; but finding no way to bring him in because of the crowd, they went up on the roof and let him down with his bed through the tiles into the middle of the crowd in front of Jesus. When he saw their faith, he said, "Friend, your sins are forgiven you." Then the scribes and the Pharisees began to question, "Who is this who is speaking blasphemies? Who can forgive sins but God alone?" When Jesus perceived their questionings, he answered them, "Why do you raise such questions in your hearts? Which is easier, to say, 'Your sins are forgiven you,' or to say, 'Stand up and walk'? But so that you may know that the Son of Man has authority on earth to forgive sins" - he said to the one who was paralyzed - "I say to you, stand up and take your bed and go to your home." Immediately he stood up before them, took what he had been lying on, and went to his home, glorifying God.

Be grateful for God's compassion expressed in the faith of your friends. Be grateful for the faith of your friends. And give your friends cause to be grateful for your faith.

Epistle

II TIMOTHY 1:6-7 For this reason I remind you to rekindle the gift of God that is within you through the laying on of my hands; for God did not give us a spirit of cowardice, but rather a spirit of power and of love and of self-discipline.

II TIMOTHY 2:14, 23-25 Remind them of this, and warn them before God that they are to avoid wrangling over words, which does no good but only ruins those who are listening. Have nothing to do with stupid and senseless controversies; you know that they breed quarrels. And the Lord's servant must not be quarrelsome but kindly to everyone, an apt teacher, patient, correcting opponents with gentleness.

What is it to heal if not to distinguish a new present from the past? What is it to forgive if not to distinguish a new present from the past? Take then every opportunity to heal and to forgive yourself and those around you, to help all of you distinguish a new present from the past.

Psalm

PSALM 33:1-9, 11, 13-15, 18, 20-22 Rejoice in the LORD, O ye righteous: for praise is comely for the upright. Praise the LORD with harp: sing unto him with the psaltery and an instrument of ten strings. Sing unto him a new song; play skillfully with a loud noise. For the word of the LORD is right; and all his works are done in truth. He loveth righteousness: the earth is full of the goodness of the LORD. By the word of the LORD were the heavens made; and all the host of them by the breath of his mouth. He gathereth the waters of the sea together as an heap: he layeth up the depth in storehouses. Let all the earth [regard the LORD with wonder:] let all the inhabitants of the world stand in awe of him. For he spake, and it was done; he commanded, and it stood fast. The counsel of the LORD standeth for ever, the thoughts of his heart to all generations. The LORD looketh from heaven; he beholdeth all the sons of men. From the place of his habitation he looketh upon all the inhabitants of the earth. He fashioneth their hearts alike; he considereth all their works. Behold, the eye of the LORD is upon them that [regard him with wonder,] upon them that hope in his mercy. Our soul waiteth for the LORD: he is our help and our shield. For our heart shall rejoice in him, because we have trusted in his holy name. Let thy mercy, O LORD, be upon us, according as we hope in thee.

Quiet

Prayer

O Birther! Father-Mother of the Cosmos,

Focus your light within us - make it useful:

Create your reign of unity now -

Your one desire then acts with ours,
as in all light, so in all forms.

Grant what we need each day in bread and insight.

Loose the cords of mistakes binding us,
as we release the strand we hold
of others' guilt.

Don't let surface things delude us,

But free us from what holds us back.

From you is born all ruling will,
the power and the life to do,
the song that beautifies all,
from age to age it renews.

Truly - power to these statements -
may they be the ground from which all
my actions grow: Amen.

                        Translated from Aramaic by Neil Douglas-Klotz[1]

Benediction

Be the Lord's heart and hands in the world today.

Tuesday

Day

Introit

Look, not again, but for the first time. What have you not seen?

Gospel

MATTHEW 20:29-34 As they were leaving Jericho, a large crowd followed him. There were two blind men sitting by the roadside. When they heard that Jesus was passing by, they shouted, "Lord, have mercy on us, Son of David!" The crowd sternly ordered them to be quiet; but they shouted even more loudly, "Have mercy on us, Lord, Son of David!" Jesus stood still and called them, saying, "What do you want me to do for you?" They said to him, "Lord, let our eyes be opened." Moved with compassion, Jesus touched their eyes. Immediately they regained their sight and followed him.

JOHN 9:1, 6-39 As he walked along, he saw a man blind from birth. ...he spat on the ground and made mud with the saliva and spread the mud on the man's eyes, saying to him, "Go, wash in the pool of Siloam" (which means Sent). Then he went and washed and came back able to see. The neighbors and those who had seen him before as a beggar began to ask, "Is this not the man who used to sit and beg?" Some were saying, "It is he." Others were saying, "No, but it is someone like him." He kept saying, "I am the man." But they kept asking him, "Then how were your eyes opened?" He answered, "The man called Jesus made mud, spread it on my eyes, and said to me, 'Go to Siloam and wash.' Then I went and washed and received my sight." They said to him, "Where is he?" He said, "I do not know." They brought to the Pharisees the man who had formerly been blind. Now it was a sabbath day when Jesus made the mud and opened his eyes. Then the Pharisees also began to ask him how he had received his sight. He said to them, "He put mud on my eyes. Then I washed, and now I see."

Some of the Pharisees said, "This man is not from God, for he does not observe the sabbath." But others said, "How can a man who is a sinner perform such signs?" And they were divided. So they said again to the blind man, "What do you say about him? It was your eyes he opened." He said, "He is a prophet."

The Jews did not believe that he had been blind and had received his sight until they called the parents of the man who had received his sight and asked them, "Is this your son, who you say was born blind? How then does he now see?" His parents answered, "We know that this is our son, and that he was born blind; but we do not know how it is that now he sees, nor do we know who opened his eyes. Ask him; he is of age. He will speak for himself." His parents said this because they were afraid of the Jews; for the Jews had already agreed that anyone who confessed Jesus to be the Messiah would be put out of the synagogue. Therefore his parents said, "He is of age; ask him." So for the second time they called the man who had been blind, and they said to him, "Give glory to God! We know that this man is a sinner." He answered, "I do not know whether he is a sinner. One thing I do know, that though I was blind, now I see." They said to him, "What did he do to you? How did he open your eyes?" He answered them, "I have told you already, and you would not listen. Why do you want to hear it again? Do you also want to become his disciples?" Then they reviled him, saying, "You are his disciple, but we are disciples of Moses. We know that God has spoken to Moses, but as for this man, we do not know where he comes from." The man answered, "Here is an astonishing thing! You do not know where he comes from, and yet he opened my eyes. We know that God does not listen to sinners, but he does listen to one who worships him and obeys his will. Never since the world began has it been heard that anyone opened the eyes of a person born blind. If this man were not from God, he could do nothing." They answered him, "You were born entirely in sins, and are you trying to teach us?" And they drove him out.

Jesus heard that they had driven him out, and when he found him, he said, "Do you believe in the Son of Man?" He answered, "And who is he, sir? Tell me, so that I may believe in him." Jesus said to him, "You have seen him, and the one speaking with you is he." He said, "Lord, I believe." And he worshiped him. Jesus said, "I came into this world for judgment so that those who do not see may see, and those who do see may become blind." Some of the Pharisees near him heard this and said to him, "Surely we are not blind are we?" Jesus said to them, "If you were blind, you would not have sin. But that you say, 'We see,' your sin remains."

Consider that the arrogance of certainty makes and keeps you blind. About whom and about what might you be arrogantly certain?

Epistle

JAMES 1:19-27 You must understand this, my beloved: let everyone be quick to listen, slow to speak, slow to anger; for your anger does not produce God's righteousness. Therefore rid yourselves of all sordidness and rank growth of wickedness, and welcome with meekness the implanted word that has the power to save your souls. But be doers of the word, and not merely hearers who deceive themselves. For if any are hearers of the word and not doers, they are like those who look at themselves in a mirror; for they look at themselves and, on going away, immediately forget what they were like. But those who look into the perfect law, the law of liberty, and persevere, being not hearers who forget but doers who act - they will be blessed in their doing.

If any think they are religious, and do not bridle their tongues but deceive their hearts, their religion is worthless. Religion that is pure and undefiled before God, the Father, is this: to care for widows and orphans in their distress, and to keep oneself unstained by the world.

Psalm

PSALM 111:1-4, 7-10 Praise ye the LORD. I will praise the LORD with my whole heart, in the assembly of the upright, and in the congregation. The works of the LORD are great, sought out of all them that have pleasure therein. His work is honourable and glorious: and his righteousness endureth for ever. He hath made his wonderful works to be remembered: the LORD is gracious and full of compassion. The works of his hands are verity and judgment; all his commandments are sure. They stand fast for ever and ever, and are done in truth and uprightness. He sent redemption unto his people: he hath commanded his covenant for ever: holy and reverend is his name. [Regarding the LORD with awe and wonder] is the beginning of wisdom: a good understanding have all they that do his commandments: his praise endureth for ever.

Quiet

Prayer

God be in my head, and in my understanding;
God be in my eyes, and in my looking;
God be in my mouth, and in my speaking;
God be in my heart, and in my thinking.
God be at my end, and at my departing.

                                    Old Sarum Primer[2]

Benediction

As you continue your day, offer up to him whom you serve your understanding, your looking, your speaking, your thinking, and your doing, so that your life will be complete in every moment and at your departing.

Tuesday

Evening

Introit

JAMES 2:8 You do well if you really fulfill the royal law according to the scripture, "You shall love your neighbor as yourself."

Gospel

LUKE 7:36-50 One of the Pharisees asked Jesus to eat with him, and he went into the Pharisee's house and took his place at the table. And a woman in the city, who was a sinner, having learned that he was eating in the Pharisee's house, brought an alabaster jar of ointment. She stood behind him at his feet, weeping, and began to bathe his feet with her tears and to dry them with her hair. Then she continued kissing his feet and anointing them with the ointment. Now when the Pharisee who had invited him saw it, he said to himself, "If this man were a prophet, he would have known who and what kind of woman this is who is touching him - that she is a sinner." Jesus spoke up and said to him, "Simon, I have something to say to you." "Teacher," he replied, "Speak." Jesus said, "A certain creditor had two debtors; one owed five hundred denarii, and the other fifty. When they could not pay, he canceled the debts for both of them. Now which of them will love him more?" Simon answered, "I suppose the one for whom he canceled the greater debt." And Jesus said to him, "You have judged rightly." Then turning toward the woman, he said to Simon, "Do you see this woman? I entered your house; you gave me no water for my feet, but she has bathed my feet with her tears and dried them with her hair. You gave me no kiss, but from the time I came in she has not stopped kissing my feet. You did not anoint my head with oil, but she has anointed my feet with ointment. Therefore, I tell you, her sins, which were many, have been forgiven; hence she has shown great love. But the one to whom little is forgiven, loves little." Then he said to her, "Your sins are forgiven." But those who were at the table with him began to say among themselves, "Who is this who even forgives sins?" And he said to the woman, "Your faith has saved you; go in peace."

Epistle

JAMES 2:1-6, 8 My brothers and sisters, do you with your acts of favoritism really believe in our glorious Lord Jesus Christ? For if a person with gold rings and in fine clothes comes into your assembly, and if a poor person in dirty clothes also comes in, and if you take notice of the one wearing the fine clothes and say, "Have a seat here, please," while to the one who is poor you say, "Stand there," or, "Sit at my feet," have you not made distinctions among yourselves, and become judges with evil thoughts? Listen, my beloved brothers and sisters. Has not God chosen the poor in the world to be rich in faith and to be heirs of the kingdom that he has promised to those who love him? But you have dishonored the poor. Is it not the rich who oppress you? Is it not they who drag you into court? Is it not they who blaspheme the excellent name that was invoked over you? You do well if you really fulfill the royal law according to the scripture, "You shall love your neighbor as yourself."

Psalm

PSALM 139:1-18, 23-24   O LORD, thou hast searched me, and known me. Thou knowest my downsitting and mine uprising, thou understandest my thought afar off. Thou compassest my path and my lying down, and art acquainted with all my ways. For there is not a word in my tongue, but, lo, O LORD, thou knowest it altogether. Thou hast beset me behind and before, and laid thine hand upon me. Such knowledge is too wonderful for me; it is high, I cannot attain unto it. Whither shall I go from thy spirit? or whither shall I flee from thy presence? If I ascend up into heaven, thou art there: if I make my bed in hell, behold, thou art there. If I take the wings of the morning, and dwell in the uttermost parts of the sea; Even there shall thy hand lead me, and thy right hand shall hold me. If I say, Surely the darkness shall cover me; even the night shall be light about me. Yea, the darkness hideth not from thee; but the night shineth as the day: the darkness and the light are both alike to thee. For thou hast possessed my reins: thou hast covered me in my mother's womb. I will praise thee; for I am wonderfully made: marvelous are thy works; and that my soul knoweth right well. My substance was not hid from thee, when I was made in secret, and curiously wrought in the lowest parts of the earth. Thine eyes did see my substance, yet being unperfect; and in thy book all my members were written, which in continuance were fashioned, when as yet there was none of them. How precious also are thy thoughts unto me, O God! how great is the sum of them! If I should count them, they are more in number than the sand: when I awake, I am still with thee. Search me, O God, and know my heart: try me, and know my thoughts: and lead me in the way everlasting.

Quiet Prayer

Heavenly Father, thank you for your gifts of generosity and forgiveness. Help me to be as extravagant as you in sharing them. Amen.

Benediction

LUKE 7:47 "I tell you, her sins, which were many, have been forgiven; hence she has shown great love."

Whatever you think of your sins, go and show great love.

Tuesday

Night

Introit

Whom will you follow? Whom will you serve?

Gospel

LUKE 7:18-22 So John summoned two of his disciples and sent them to the Lord to ask, "Are you the one who is to come, or are we to wait for another?" When the men had come to him, they said, "John the Baptist has sent us to you to ask, 'Are you the one who is to come, or are we to wait for another?'" Jesus had just then cured many people of diseases, plagues, and evil spirits, and had given sight to many who were blind. And he answered them, "Go and tell John what you have seen and heard: the blind receive their sight, the lame walk, the lepers are cleansed, the deaf hear, the dead are raised, the poor have good news brought to them."

Be done with asking and waiting. It is time to follow Jesus.

Epistle

EPHESIANS 5:1-2, 8-10, 18-21 Therefore be imitators of God, as beloved children, and live in love, as Christ loved us and gave himself up for us... For once you were darkness, but now in the Lord you are light. Live as children of light - for the fruit of the light is found in all that is good and right and true. Try to find out what is pleasing to the Lord. …be filled with the Spirit, as you sing psalms and hymns and spiritual songs among yourselves, singing and making melody to the Lord in your hearts, giving thanks to God the Father at all times and for everything in the name of our Lord Jesus Christ. Be subject to one another out of reverence for Christ.

Psalm

PSALM 145:1-21 I will extol thee, my God, O king; and I will bless thy name for ever and ever. Every day will I bless thee; and I will praise thy name for ever and ever. Great is the LORD, and greatly to be praised; and his greatness is unsearchable. One generation shall praise thy works to another, and shall declare thy mighty acts. I will speak of the glorious honour of thy majesty, and of thy wondrous works. And men shall speak of [thy might] and I will declare thy greatness. They shall abundantly utter the memory of thy great goodness, and shall sing of thy righteousness. The LORD is gracious, and full of compassion; slow to anger, and of great mercy. The LORD is good to all: and his tender mercies are over all his works. All thy works shall praise thee, O LORD; and thy saints shall bless thee. They shall speak of the glory of thy kingdom, and talk of thy power; To make known to the sons of men his mighty acts, and the glorious majesty of his kingdom. Thy kingdom is an everlasting kingdom, and thy dominion endureth throughout all generations. The LORD upholdeth all that fall, and raiseth up all those that be bowed down. The eyes of all wait upon thee; and thou givest them their meat in due season. Thou openest thine hand, and satisfiest the desire of every living thing. The LORD is righteous in all his ways, and holy in all his works. The LORD is nigh unto all them that call upon him, to all that call upon him in truth. He will fulfill the desire of them that [regard him with wonder:] he also will hear their cry, and will save them. The LORD preserveth all them that love him... My mouth shall speak the praise of the LORD: and let all flesh bless his holy name forever and ever.

Quiet

Prayer

Thanks for the gift of today!
Thanks for the hope and uncertainty of tomorrow!
Thanks for this time of rest!
Thanks!

Benediction

EPHESIANS 5:1-2, 8-10 Therefore be imitators of God, as beloved children, and live in love, as Christ loved us and gave himself up for us... For once you were darkness, but now in the Lord you are light. Live as children of light - for the fruit of the light is found in all that is good and right and true. Try to find out what is pleasing to the Lord.

And now, sleep as a child of light.

Wednesday

Wednesday

Morning

Introit

Thanks for this time of rest!
Thanks for the hope and uncertainty of today!
Thanks for the gift of today!
Thanks!

Gospel

MATTHEW 10:1-5, 7-10 Then Jesus summoned his twelve disciples and gave them authority over unclean spirits, to cast them out, and to cure every disease and every sickness. These are the names of the twelve apostles: first, Simon, also known as Peter, and his brother Andrew; James son of Zebedee, and his brother John; Philip and Bartholomew; Thomas and Matthew the tax collector; James son of Alphaeus, and Thaddaeus; Simon the Cananaean, and Judas Iscariot, the one who betrayed him. These twelve Jesus sent out with the following instructions:

"As you go, proclaim the good news, 'The kingdom of heaven has come near.' Cure the sick, raise the dead, cleanse the lepers, cast out demons. You received without payment; give without payment. Take no gold, or silver, or copper in your belts, no bag for your journey, or two tunics, or sandals, or a staff; for laborers deserve their food."

And how shall we consider the kingdom of heaven?

MATTHEW 13:31-33, 45-46 He put before them another parable: "The kingdom of heaven is like a mustard seed that someone took and sowed in his field; it is the smallest of all the seeds, but when it has grown it is the greatest of shrubs and becomes a tree, so that the birds of the air come and make nests in its branches." He told them another parable: "The kingdom of heaven is like yeast that a woman took and mixed it with three measures of flour until all of it was leavened. Again, the kingdom of heaven is like a merchant in search of fine pearls; on finding one pearl of great value, he went and sold all that he had and bought it."

And how shall we consider being a disciple of Jesus?

MATTHEW 16:24-26 Then Jesus told his disciples, "If any want to become my followers, let them deny themselves and take up their cross and follow me. For those who want to save their life will lose it, and those who lose their life for my sake will find it. For what will it profit them if they gain the whole world but forfeit their life? Or what will they give in return for their life?"

Epistle

Therefore in every day, in every hour, in every moment…

EPHESIANS 5:1-2, 8-10, 18-21 …be imitators of God, as beloved children, and live in love, as Christ loved us and gave himself up for us... For once you were darkness, but now in the Lord you are light. Live as children of light - for the fruit of the light is found in all that is good and right and true. Try to find out what is pleasing to the Lord. …be filled with the Spirit, as you sing psalms and hymns and spiritual songs among yourselves, singing and making melody to the Lord in your hearts, giving thanks to God the Father at all times and for everything in the name of our Lord Jesus Christ. Be subject to one another out of reverence for Christ.

Psalm

PSALM 19:1-10, 14 The heavens declare the glory of God; and the firmament sheweth his handywork. Day unto day uttereth speech, and night unto night sheweth knowledge. There is no speech nor language, where their voice is not heard. Their line is gone out through all the earth, and their words to the end of the world. In them hath he set a tabernacle for the sun, Which is as a bridegroom coming out of his chamber, and rejoiceth as a strong man to run a race. His going forth is from the end of the heaven, and his circuit unto the ends of it: and there is nothing hid from the heat thereof. The law of the LORD is perfect, converting the soul: the testimony of the LORD is sure, making wise the simple. The statutes of the LORD are right, rejoicing the heart: the commandment of the LORD is pure, enlightening the eyes …the judgments of the LORD are true and righteous altogether. More to be desired are they than gold, yea, than much fine gold: sweeter also than honey and the honeycomb. Moreover by them is thy servant warned: and in keeping them there is great reward. Who can understand his errors? cleanse thou me from secret faults. Keep back thy servant also from presumptuous sins; let them not have dominion over me: then shall I be upright, and I shall be innocent from the great transgression. Let the words of my mouth, and the meditation of my heart, be acceptable in thy sight, O LORD, my strength, and my redeemer.

Not only the words of my mouth and the meditation of my heart, but especially all that I do; while all that I do may be divinely tolerated, may all that I do be acceptable in thy sight, O LORD, my strength, and my redeemer.

Quiet Prayer

Our Father who art in Heaven, hallowed be Thy name. Thy Kingdom come. Thy will be done on earth, as it is in Heaven. Give us this day our daily bread. And forgive us our trespasses, as we forgive those who trespass against us. And lead us not into temptation, but deliver us from evil. For Thine is the Kingdom, and the power and the glory for ever. Amen.

Benediction

PHILIPPIANS 4:8 Finally, beloved, whatever is true, whatever is honorable, whatever is just, whatever is pure, whatever is pleasing, whatever is commendable, if there is any excellence and if there is anything worthy of praise, think about these things.

Wednesday

Day

Introit

Do not force yourself to understand God.
You'll just hurt yourself.

Gospel

MARK 6:34-44 As he went ashore, he saw a great crowd; and he had compassion for them, because they were like sheep without a shepherd; and he began to teach them many things. When it grew late, his disciples came to him and said, "This is a deserted place, and the hour is now very late; send them away so that they may go into the surrounding country and villages and buy something for themselves to eat." But he answered them, "You give them something to eat." They said to him, "Are we to go and buy two hundred denarii worth of bread, and give it to them to eat?" And he said to them, "How many loaves have you? Go and see." When they had found out, they said, "Five, and two fish." Then he ordered them to get all the people to sit down in groups on the green grass. So they sat down in groups of hundreds and of fifties. Taking the five loaves and the two fish, he looked up to heaven, and blessed and broke the loaves, and gave them to his disciples to set before the people; and he divided the two fish among them all. And all ate and were filled; and they took up twelve baskets full of broken pieces and of the fish. Those who had eaten the loaves numbered more than five thousand.

MARK 8:1-21 In those days when there was again a great crowd without anything to eat, he called his disciples and said to them, "I have compassion for the crowd, because they have been with me now for three days and have nothing to eat. If I send them away hungry to their homes, they will faint on the way - and some of them have come from a great distance." His disciples replied, "How can one feed these people with bread here in the desert?" He asked them, "How many loaves do you have?" They said, "Seven." Then he ordered the crowd to sit down on the ground; and he took the seven loaves, and after giving thanks he broke them and gave them to his disciples to distribute; and they distributed them to the crowd. They had also a few small fish; and after blessing them, he ordered that these too should be distributed. They ate and were filled; and they took up the broken pieces left over, seven baskets full. Now there were about four thousand people. And he sent them away. And immediately he got into the boat with his disciples and went to the district of Dalmanutha.

The Pharisees came and began to argue with him, asking him for a sign from heaven, to test him. And he sighed deeply in his spirit and said, "Why does this generation ask for a sign? Truly I tell you, no sign will be given to this generation." And he left them, and getting into the boat again, he went across to the other side.

Now the disciples had forgotten to bring any bread; and they had only one loaf with them in the boat. And he cautioned them, saying, "Watch out - beware of the yeast of the Pharisees and the yeast of Herod." They said to one another, "It is because we have no bread." And becoming aware of it, Jesus said to them, "Why are you talking about having no bread? Do you still not perceive or understand? Are your hearts hardened? Do you have eyes, and fail to see? Do you have ears, and fail to hear? And do you not remember? When I broke the five loaves for the five thousand, how many baskets full of broken pieces did you collect?" They said to him, "Twelve." Then he asked, "And the seven for the four thousand, how many baskets full of broken pieces did you collect?" And they said to him, "Seven." Then he said to them, "Do you not yet understand?"

What is it that you do not yet understand, or appreciate, or whatever, that you think is necessary to bring about the good that you want?

Epistle

PHILIPPIANS 4:4-7 Rejoice in the Lord always; again I will say, Rejoice. Let your gentleness be known to everyone. The Lord is near. Do not worry about anything, but in everything by prayer and supplication with thanksgiving let your requests be made known to God. And the peace of God, which surpasses all understanding, will guard your hearts and your minds in Christ Jesus.

Psalm

PSALM 104:1-35 Bless the LORD, O my soul. O LORD my God, thou art very great; thou art clothed with honour and majesty. Who coverest thyself with light as with a garment: who stretchest out the heavens like a curtain: Who layeth the beams of his chambers in the waters: who maketh the clouds his chariot: who walketh upon the wings of the wind: Who maketh his angels spirits; his ministers a flaming fire: Who laid the foundations of the earth, that it should not be removed for ever. Thou coveredst it with the deep as with a garment: the waters stood above the mountains. At thy rebuke they fled; at the voice of thy thunder they hasted away. They go up by the mountains; they go down by the valleys unto the place which thou hast founded for them. Thou hast set a bound that they may not pass over; that they turn not again to cover the earth. He sendeth the springs into the valleys, which run among the hills. They give drink to every beast of the field: the wild asses quench their thirst. By them shall the fowls of the heaven have their habitation, which sing among the branches. He watereth the hills from his chambers: the earth is satisfied with the fruit of thy works. He causeth the grass to grow for the cattle, and herb for the service of man: that he may bring forth food out of the earth; And wine that maketh glad the heart of man, and oil to make his face to shine, and bread which strengtheneth man's heart. The trees of the LORD are full of sap; the cedars of Lebanon, which he hath planted; Where the birds make their nests: as for the stork, the fir trees are her house. The high hills are a refuge for the wild goats; and the rocks for the conies. He appointed the moon for seasons:

the sun knoweth his going down. Thou makest darkness, and it is night: wherein all the beasts of the forest do creep forth. The young lions roar after their prey, and seek their meat from God. The sun ariseth, they gather themselves together, and lay them down in their dens. Man goeth forth unto his work and to his labour until the evening. O LORD, how manifold are thy works! in wisdom hast thou made them all: the earth is full of thy riches. So is this great and wide sea, wherein are things creeping innumerable, both small and great beasts. There go the ships: there is that leviathan, whom thou hast made to play therein. These wait all upon thee; that thou mayest give them their meat in due season. That thou givest them they gather: thou openest thine hand, they are filled with good. Thou hidest thy face, they are troubled: thou takest away their breath, they die, and return to their dust. Thou sendest forth thy spirit, they are created: and thou renewest the face of the earth. The glory of the LORD shall endure forever: the LORD shall rejoice in his works. He looketh on the earth, and it trembleth: he toucheth the hills, and they smoke. I will sing unto the LORD as long as I live: I will sing praise to my God while I have my being. My meditation of him shall be sweet: I will be glad in the LORD. ...Bless thou the LORD, O my soul. Praise ye the LORD.

Quiet

Prayer

Thou
Who art beyond my knowing
And whose child I am,
Thou
Who art beyond my knowing
And who has granted me
To have joy and sorrow in Thy mystery,
Thou...

Benediction

Understanding may be helpful for contribution and service, but it is not sufficient. Also, wonder and commitment can be useful. However, and certainly, persistence in the face of uncertainty will be required.

Wednesday

Evening

Introit

You want to follow Jesus and you are unsure and afraid. But if not here, where? If not now, when? What to do?

Gospel

MATTHEW 14:22-31 Immediately [after feeding the more than five thousand,] he made the disciples get into the boat and go on ahead to the other side, while he dismissed the crowds. And after he had dismissed the crowds, he went up the mountain by himself to pray. When evening came, he was there alone, but by this time the boat, battered by the waves, was far from the land, for the wind was against them. And early in the morning he came walking toward them on the sea. But when the disciples saw him walking on the sea, they were terrified, saying, "It is a ghost!" And they cried out in fear. But immediately Jesus spoke to them and said, "Take heart, it is I; do not be afraid." Peter answered him, "Lord, if it is you, command me to come to you on the water." He said, "Come." So Peter got out of the boat, started walking on the water, and came toward Jesus. But when he noticed the strong wind, he became frightened, and beginning to sink, he cried out, "Lord, save me!" Jesus immediately reached out his hand and caught him, saying to him, "You of little faith, why did you doubt?"

Epistle

I JOHN 2:6 …whoever says, "I abide in him," ought to walk just as he walked.

And, even knowing that you are going to sink, keep walking and reaching out to Jesus.[1]

Psalm

PSALM 119:129-133, 135 Thy testimonies are wonderful: therefore doth my soul keep them. The entrance of thy words giveth light; it giveth understanding unto the simple. I opened my mouth, and panted: for I longed for thy commandments. Look thou upon me, and be merciful unto me, as thou usest to do unto those that love thy name. Order my steps in thy word: and let not any iniquity have dominion over me. Make thy face to shine upon thy servant; and teach me thy statutes.

Quiet

Prayer

O Lord, help me to keep letting go of the ordinary way of looking at life. Amen.

Benediction

MATTHEW 14:29 He said, "Come." So Peter got out of the boat, started walking on the water, and came toward Jesus.

Now it is your turn. Get out of the boat. Start walking and keep reaching out to Jesus. And, even knowing that you are going to sink, keep walking and reaching out to Jesus.

Wednesday

Night

Introit

Precious Lord, take my hand, lead me on, let me stand,
I am tired, I am weak, I am worn;
Through the storm, through the night, lead me on to the light;
Take my hand, precious Lord, lead me home.

Thomas Dorsey[2]

Gospel

MARK 5:1-20 They came to the other side of the sea, to the country of the Gerasenes. And when he had stepped out of the boat, immediately a man out of the tombs with an unclean spirit met him. He lived among the tombs; and no one could restrain him any more, even with a chain; for he had often been restrained with shackles and chains, but the chains he wrenched apart, and the shackles he broke in pieces; and no one had the strength to subdue him. Night and day among the tombs and on the mountains he was always howling and bruising himself with stones. When he saw Jesus from a distance, he ran and bowed down before him; and he shouted at the top of his voice, "What have you to do with me, Jesus, Son of the Most High God? I adjure you by God, do not torment me." For he had said to him, "Come out of the man, you unclean spirit!" Then Jesus asked him, "What is your name?" He replied, "My name is Legion; for we are many." He begged him earnestly not to send them out of the country. Now there on the hillside a great herd of swine was feeding; and the unclean spirits begged him, "Send us into the swine; let us enter them." So he gave them permission. And the unclean spirits came out and entered the swine; and the herd, numbering about two thousand, rushed down the steep bank into the sea, and were drowned in the sea. The swineherds ran off and told it in the city and in the country. Then people came to see what it was that had happened. They came to Jesus and saw the demoniac sitting there, clothed and in his right mind, the very man who had had the "legion"; and they were afraid. Those who had seen what had happened to the demoniac and to the swine reported it. Then they began to beg Jesus to leave their neighborhood. As he was getting into the boat, the man who had been possessed by demons begged him that he might be with him. But Jesus refused, and said to him, "Go home to your friends, and tell them how much the Lord has done for you, and what mercy he has shown you." And he went away and began to proclaim in the Decapolis how much Jesus had done for him; and everyone was amazed.

Epistle

I JOHN 4:18 There is no fear in love, but perfect love casts out fear...

I CORINTHIANS 16:14 Let all that you do be done in love.

Psalm

PSALM 147:1-3, 6-9, 11-14, 20 Praise ye the LORD: for it is good to sing praises unto our God; for it is pleasant; and praise is comely. The LORD doth build up Jerusalem: he gathereth together the outcasts of Israel. He healeth the broken in heart, and bindeth up their wounds. The LORD lifteth up the meek: he casteth the wicked down to the ground. Sing unto the LORD with thanksgiving; sing praise upon the harp unto our God: Who covereth the heaven with clouds, who prepareth rain for the earth, who maketh grass to grow upon the mountains. He giveth to the beast his food, and to the young ravens that cry. The LORD taketh pleasure in them that [regard him with wonder,] in those that hope in his mercy. Praise the LORD, O Jerusalem; praise thy God, O Zion. ... he hath blessed thy children within thee. He maketh peace in thy borders, and filleth thee with the finest of the wheat. Praise ye the LORD.

Quiet

Prayer

Lord, make me an instrument of your peace.

Where there is hatred, let me sow love;

Where there is injury, pardon;

Where there is doubt, faith;

Where there is despair, hope;

Where there is darkness, light;

Where there is sadness, joy.

O divine Master, grant that I may not so much seek

To be consoled, as to console,

To be understood, as to understand,

To be loved, as to love,

For it is in giving that we receive;

It is in pardoning that we are pardoned;

It is in dying that we are born to eternal life.

Possibly Fr. Esther Bouquerel[3]

Benediction

And for tonight, precious Lord, thank you for bringing me home.

Thursday

Thursday

Morning

Introit

Take, Lord, unto Thyself,
My sense of self: and let it vanish utterly:

Take, Lord, my life,
Live Thou Thy life through me:

I live no longer, Lord,
But in me now
Thou livest:

Aye, between Thee and me, my God,
There is no longer room for "I" and "mine."

Tukaram[1]

Gospel

MARK 9:33-37 Then they came to Capernaum; and when he was in the house he asked them, "What were you arguing about on the way?" But they were silent, for on the way they had argued with one another who was the greatest. He sat down, called the twelve, and said to them, "Whoever wants to be first must be last of all and servant of all." Then he took a little child and put it among them; and taking it in his arms, he said to them, "Whoever welcomes one such child in my name welcomes me, and whoever welcomes me welcomes not me but the one who sent me."

MARK 10:13-16 People were bringing little children to him in order that he might touch them; and the disciples spoke sternly to them. But when Jesus saw this, he was indignant and said to them, "Let the little children come to me; do not stop them; for it is to such as these that the kingdom of God belongs. Truly I tell you, whoever does not receive the kingdom of God as a little child will never enter it." And he took them up in his arms, laid his hands on them, and blessed them.

MARK 10:35-38, 41-45 James and John, the sons of Zebedee, came forward to him and said to him, "Teacher, we want you to do for us whatever we ask of you." And he said to them, "What is it you want me to do for you?" And they said to him, "Grant us to sit, one at your right hand and one at your left, in your glory." But Jesus said to them, "You do not know what you are asking."

When the ten heard this, they began to be angry with James and John. So Jesus called them and said to them, "You know that among the Gentiles those whom they recognize as their rulers lord it over them, and their great ones are tyrants over them. But it is not so among you; but whoever wishes to become great among you must be your servant, and whoever wishes to be first among you must be slave of all. For the Son of Man came not to be served but to serve, and to give his life a ransom for many."

Epistle

PHILIPPIANS 2:1-5 If then there is any encouragement in Christ, any consolation from love, any sharing in the Spirit, any compassion and sympathy, make my joy complete: be of the same mind, having the same love, being in full accord and of one mind. Do nothing from selfish ambition or conceit, but in humility regard others as better than yourselves. Let each of you look not to your own interests, but to the interests of others. Let the same mind be in you that was in Christ Jesus…

Psalm

PSALM 119:33-37 Teach me, O LORD, the way of thy statutes; and I shall keep it unto the end. Give me understanding, and I shall keep thy law; yea, I shall observe it with my whole heart. Make me to go in the path of thy commandments; for therein do I delight. Incline my heart unto thy testimonies, and not to covetousness. Turn away mine eyes from beholding vanity; and quicken thou me in thy way.

Quiet

Prayer

Source of all that is,
Thank you for the gift of all that is.
Help us to share it with all those around us.

Thank you for the gift of love: friendship, joy and compassion.
Help us to share it with all those around us.

Thank you for the gift of our daily bread and all that sustains us.
Help us to share it with all those around us.

Thank you for the gift of forgiveness so that we might let go of our claims on each other.
Help us to share it with all those around us.

Thank you for the gift of your presence and comfort in adversity.
Help us to share it with all those around us.

Thank you for the gift of possibility for the future.
Help us to share it with all those around us. Let it be so and Amen.

Benediction

Hope for the time when nobody knows that is was you who did all those wonderful, marvelous, terrific things. Hope for the time when everybody appreciates only all those wonderful, marvelous, terrific things.

Thursday

Day

Introit

The authentic answer to "Who is my neighbor?" will almost always be inconvenient and sometimes even dangerous. And faith without works is dead.

Gospel

MARK 12:28-34 One of the scribes came near and heard them disputing with one another, and seeing that he answered them well, he asked him, "Which commandment is the first of all?" Jesus answered, "The first is, 'Hear, O Israel: the Lord our God, the Lord is one; you shall love the Lord your God with all your heart, and with all your soul, and with all your mind, and with all your strength.' The second is this, 'You shall love your neighbor as yourself.' There is no other commandment greater than these." Then the scribe said to him, "You are right, Teacher; you have truly said that 'he is one, and besides him there is no other'; and 'to love him with all the heart, and with all the understanding, and with all the strength,' and 'to love one's neighbor as oneself,' - this is much more important than all whole burnt offerings and sacrifices." When Jesus saw that he answered wisely, he said to him, "You are not far from the kingdom of God."

LUKE 10:25-37 Just then a lawyer stood up to test Jesus. "Teacher," he said, "what must I do to inherit eternal life?" He said to him, "What is written in the law? What do you read there?" He answered, "You shall love the Lord your God with all your heart, and with all your soul, and with all your strength, and with all your mind; and your neighbor as yourself." And he said to him, "You have given the right answer; do this, and you will live." But wanting to justify himself, he asked Jesus, "And who is my neighbor?" Jesus replied, "A man was going down from Jerusalem to Jericho, and fell into the hands of robbers, who stripped him, beat him, and went away, leaving him half dead. Now by chance a priest was going down that road; and when he saw him, he passed by on the other side. So likewise a Levite, when he came to the place and saw him, passed by on the other side. But a Samaritan while traveling came near him; and when he saw him, he was moved with pity. He went to him and bandaged his wounds, having poured oil and wine on them. Then he put him on his own animal, brought him to an inn, and took care of him. The next day he took out two denarii, gave them to the innkeeper, and said, 'Take care of him; and when I come back, I will repay you whatever more you spend.' Which of these three, do you think, was a neighbor to the man who fell into the hands of the robbers?" He said, "The one who showed him mercy." Jesus said to him, "Go and do likewise."

Epistle

JAMES 2:14-17, 26 What good is it, my brothers and sisters, if you say you have faith but do not have works? If a brother or sister is naked and lacks daily food, and one of you says to them, "Go in peace; keep warm and eat your fill," and yet you do not supply their bodily needs, what is the good of that? So faith by itself, if it has no works, is dead. For just as the body without the spirit is dead, so faith without works is also dead.

Psalm

PSALM 23:1-6 The LORD is my shepherd; I shall not want. He maketh me to lie down in green pastures: he leadeth me beside the still waters. He restoreth my soul: he leadeth me in the paths of righteousness for his name's sake. Yea, though I walk through the valley of the shadow of death, I will fear no evil: for thou art with me; thy rod and thy staff they comfort me. Thou preparest a table before me in the presence of my enemies: thou anointest my head with oil; my cup runneth over. Surely goodness and mercy shall follow me all the days of my life: and I will dwell in the house of the LORD forever.

And for this I am grateful. Now, for whom can I pay this forward? For whom can I be a shepherd?

Quiet

Prayer

Almighty God,
in whom we live and move and have our being,
you have made us for yourself,
and our hearts are restless until they find their rest in you.
Grant us purity of heart and strength of purpose,
that no selfish passion may hinder us from knowing your will;
no weakness from doing it;
but that in your light we may see light
and in your service we may find perfect freedom.

St. Augustine[2]

Benediction

At times, when you find yourself worrying about "your" holiness, consider that your worries will disappear in service.

Thursday

Evening

Introit

Consider how much of what you do is done to be noticed.

Gospel

LUKE 14:7-14 [On one occasion Jesus was going to the house of a leader of the Pharisees to eat a meal on the Sabbath.] When he noticed how the guests chose the places of honor, he told them a parable. "When you are invited by someone to a wedding banquet, do not sit down at the place of honor, in case someone more distinguished than you has been invited by your host; and the host who invited both of you may come and say to you, 'Give this person your place,' and then in disgrace you would start to take the lowest place. But when you are invited, go and sit down at the lowest place, so that when your host comes, he may say to you, 'Friend, move up higher'; then you will be honored in the presence of all who sit at the table with you. For all who exalt themselves will be humbled, and those who humble themselves will be exalted."

He said also to the one who had invited him, "When you give a luncheon or a dinner, do not invite your friends or your brothers or your relatives or rich neighbors, in case they may invite you in return, and you would be repaid. But when you give a banquet, invite the poor, the crippled, the lame, and the blind. And you will be blessed, because they cannot repay you..."

Seek out those who cannot pay you, that is, those who cannot give you anything, so that you may serve them.

Epistle

TITUS 3:1-2 Remind them...to be ready for every good work, to speak evil of no one, to avoid quarreling and boastfulness, to be gentle, and to show every courtesy to everyone.

Psalm

PSALM 119:10-16, 18, 24 With my whole heart have I sought thee: O let me not wander from thy commandments. Thy word have I hid in mine heart, that I might not sin against thee. Blessed art thou, O LORD: teach me thy statutes. With my lips have I declared all the judgments of thy mouth. I have rejoiced in the way of thy testimonies, as much as in all riches. I will meditate in thy precepts, and have respect unto thy ways. I will delight myself in thy statutes: I will not forget thy word. Open thou mine eyes, that I may behold wondrous things out of thy law. Thy testimonies also are my delight and my counsellors.

Quiet

Prayer

My Father, teach us not only thy will, but how to do it. Teach us the best way of doing the best thing, lest we spoil the end by unworthy means.

J. H. Jowett[3]

Benediction

Be compassionate, humble, and generous to demonstrate and call forth another way of being in the world, not to impress others with your capacity for compassion, humility, and generosity.

Thursday

Night

Introit

MATTHEW 18:12-14 "What do you think? If a shepherd has a hundred sheep, and one of them has gone astray, does he not leave the ninety-nine on the mountains and go in search of the one that went astray? And if he finds it, truly I tell you, he rejoices over it more than over the ninety-nine that never went astray. So it is not the will of your Father in heaven that one of these little ones should be lost."

Gospel

LUKE 15:11-32 Then Jesus said, "There was a man who had two sons. The younger of them said to his father, 'Father, give me the share of the property that will belong to me.' So he divided his property between them. A few days later the younger son gathered all he had and traveled to a distant country, and there he squandered his property in dissolute living. When he had spent everything, a severe famine took place throughout that country, and he began to be in need. So he went and hired himself out to one of the citizens of that country, who sent him to his fields to feed the pigs.

He would gladly have filled himself with the pods that the pigs were eating; and no one gave him anything. But when he came to himself he said, 'How many of my father's hired hands have bread enough and to spare, but here I am dying of hunger! I will get up and go to my father, and I will say to him, "Father, I have sinned against heaven and before you; I am no longer worthy to be called your son; treat me like one of your hired hands."' So he set off and went to his father. But while he was still far off, his father saw him and was filled with compassion; he ran and put his arms around him and kissed him. Then the son said to him, 'Father, I have sinned against heaven and before you; I am no longer worthy to be called your son.' But the father said to his slaves, 'Quickly, bring out a robe - the best one - and put it on him; put a ring on his finger and sandals on his feet. And get the fatted calf and kill it, and let us eat and celebrate; for this son of mine was dead and is alive again; he was lost and is found!' And they began to celebrate.

"Now his elder son was in the field; and when he came and approached the house, he heard music and dancing. He called one of the slaves and asked what was going on. He replied, 'Your brother has come, and your father has killed the fatted calf, because he has got him back safe and sound.' Then he became angry and refused to go in. His father came out and began to plead with him. But he answered his father, 'Listen! For all these years I have been working like a slave for you, and I have never disobeyed your command; yet you have never given me even a young goat so that I might celebrate with my friends. But when this son of yours came back, who has devoured your property with prostitutes, you killed the fatted calf for him!' Then the father said to him, 'Son, you are always with me, and all that is mine is yours. But we had to celebrate and rejoice, because this brother of yours was dead and has come to life; he was lost and has been found.'"

MATTHEW 18:21-22 Then Peter came and said to him, "Lord, if another member of the church sins against me, how often should I forgive? As many as seven times?" Jesus said to him, "Not seven times, but, I tell you, seventy-seven times."

LUKE 17:3-6 "If another disciple sins, you must rebuke the offender, and if there is repentance, you must forgive. And if the same person sins against you seven times a day, and turns back to you seven times and says, 'I repent,' you must forgive." The apostles said to the Lord, "Increase our faith!" The Lord replied, "If you had faith the size of a mustard seed, you could say to this mulberry tree, 'Be uprooted and planted in the sea,' and it would obey you."

Epistle

COLOSSIANS 3:12-17 …clothe yourselves with compassion, kindness, humility, meekness, and patience. Bear with one another and, if anyone has a complaint against another, forgive each other; just as the Lord has forgiven you, so you also must forgive. Above all, clothe yourselves with love, which binds everything together in perfect harmony. And let the peace of Christ rule in your hearts, to which indeed you were called in the one body. And be thankful. Let the word of Christ dwell in you richly; teach and admonish one another in all wisdom; and with gratitude in your hearts sing psalms, hymns, and spiritual songs to God. And whatever you do, in word or deed, do everything in the name of the Lord Jesus, giving thanks to God the Father through him.

II CORINTHIANS 2:5, 7-8 But if anyone has caused pain...you should forgive and console him, so that he may not be overwhelmed by excessive sorrow. So I urge you to reaffirm your love for him.

Psalm

PSALM 42:1-3, 5-6, 8, 11 As the hart panteth after the water brooks, so panteth my soul after thee, O God. My soul thirsteth for God, for the living God: when shall I come and appear before God? My tears have been my meat day and night… Why art thou cast down, O my soul? and why art thou disquieted in me? hope thou in God: for I shall yet praise him for the help of his countenance. O my God, my soul is cast down within me: therefore will I remember thee [of old.] Yet the LORD will command his lovingkindness in the daytime, and in the night his song shall be with me, and my prayer unto the God of my life. Why art thou cast down, O my soul? and why art thou disquieted within me? hope thou in God: for I shall yet praise him, who is the health of my countenance, and my God.

Indeed, why art thou cast down, O my soul? the LORD hath forgiven and forgotten thine iniquities![4]

Quiet

Prayer

O Lord, remember not only the men and women of good will, but also those of ill-will. But do not remember all the suffering they have inflicted on us; remember the fruits we have bought, thanks to this suffering - our comradeship, our loyalty, our humility, our courage, our generosity, the greatness of heart, which has grown out of all this, and when they come to judgment let all the fruits which we have borne be their forgiveness.

Prayer found at Ravensbrück concentration camp[5]

Benediction

O Lord, thank you for your many gifts. Thank you for your ever present mercy and goodness, and especially for the gift of forgiveness, which makes all things new. Help me to always share these with all those around me.

Friday

Friday

Morning

Introit

Money is, perhaps, the easiest greed to identify. Remind yourself that you have others.

Gospel

MATTHEW 19:16-24 Then someone came to him and said, "Teacher, what good deed must I do to have eternal life?" And he said to him, "Why do you ask me about what is good? There is only one who is good. If you wish to enter into life, keep the commandments." He said to him, "Which ones?" And Jesus said, "You shall not murder; You shall not commit adultery; You shall not steal; You shall not bear false witness; Honor your father and mother; also, You shall love your neighbor as yourself." The young man said to him, "I have kept all these; what do I still lack?" Jesus said to him, "If you wish to be perfect, go, sell your possessions, and give the money to the poor, and you will have treasure in heaven; then come, follow me." When the young man heard this word, he went away grieving, for he had many possessions. Then Jesus said to his disciples, "Truly I tell you, it will be hard for a rich person to enter the kingdom of heaven. Again I tell you, it is easier for a camel to go through the eye of a needle than for someone who is rich to enter the kingdom of God."

Consider that "eternal life," "the kingdom of heaven," and "the kingdom of God" refer to a quality of life expressed in compassionate service. Here. Now.

LUKE 16:19-31 "There was a rich man who was dressed in purple and fine linen and who feasted sumptuously every day. And at his gate lay a poor man named Lazarus, covered with sores, who longed to satisfy his hunger with what fell from the rich man's table; even the dogs would come and lick his sores. The poor man died and was carried away by the angels to be with Abraham. The rich man also died and was buried. In Hades, where he was being tormented, he looked up and saw Abraham far away with Lazarus by his side. He called out, 'Father Abraham, have mercy on me, and send Lazarus to dip the tip of his finger in water and cool my tongue; for I am in agony in these flames.' But Abraham said, 'Child, remember that during your lifetime you received your good things, and Lazarus in like manner evil things; but now he is comforted here, and you are in agony. Besides all this, between you and us a great chasm has been fixed, so that those who might want to pass from here to you cannot do so, and no one can cross from there to us.' He said, 'Then, father, I beg you to send him to my father's house - for I have five brothers - that he may warn them, so that they will not also come into this place of torment.'

Abraham replied, 'They have Moses and the prophets; they should listen to them.' He said, 'No, father Abraham; but if someone goes to them from the dead, they will repent.' He said to him, 'If they do not listen to Moses and the prophets, neither will they be convinced even if someone rises from the dead.' "

Epistle

II CORINTHIANS 9:6 The point is this: the one who sows sparingly will also reap sparingly, and the one who sows bountifully will also reap bountifully.

Psalm

PSALM 41:1 Blessed is he that [doth consider and serve the poor.]

Quiet

Prayer

Our Father in heaven, help us to honor your name. Establish your kingdom, so that all of us may walk together in your way. May what you want to have happen be done on earth as it is done in heaven. We give you thanks for our lives and our daily bread. Forgive us our debts, as we forgive our debtors and let go of our resentments against them. Lead us not into temptation, but deliver us from the evil that we and others are prone to do. And when it is necessary, protect us from ourselves. Again, and always, thank you for the gift of our lives and the opportunity therein to serve each other and you. Amen.

Benediction

Hold on to what you have with an open hand.

Friday

Day

Introit

Consider that there is no one worthy of being overlooked.

Gospel

LUKE 19:1-10 He entered Jericho and was passing through it. A man was there named Zacchaeus; he was a chief tax collector and was rich. He was trying to see who Jesus was, but on account of the crowd he could not, because he was short in stature. So he ran ahead and climbed a sycamore tree to see him, because he was going to pass that way. When Jesus came to the place, he looked up and said to him, "Zacchaeus, hurry and come down; for I must stay at your house today." So he hurried down and was happy to welcome him. All who saw it began to grumble and said, "He has gone to be the guest of one who is a sinner." Zacchaeus stood there and said to the Lord, "Look, half of my possessions, Lord, I will give to the poor; and if I have defrauded anyone of anything, I will pay back four times as much." Then Jesus said to him, "Today salvation has come to this house… For the Son of Man came to seek out and to save the lost."

Epistle

JAMES 3:13-18 Who is wise and understanding among you? Show by your good life that your works are done with gentleness born of wisdom. But if you have bitter envy and selfish ambition in your hearts, do not be boastful and false to the truth. Such wisdom does not come down from above, but is earthly, unspiritual, devilish.

For where there is envy and selfish ambition, there will also be disorder and wickedness of every kind. But the wisdom from above is first pure, then peaceable, gentle, willing to yield, full of mercy and good fruits, without a trace of partiality or hypocrisy. And a harvest of righteousness is sown in peace for those who make peace.

Psalm

PSALM 67:1-7 God be merciful unto us, and bless us; and cause his face to shine upon us; Selah. That thy way may be known upon earth, thy saving health among all nations. Let the people praise thee, O God; let all the people praise thee. O let the nations be glad and sing for joy: for thou shalt judge the people righteously, and govern the nations upon earth. Selah. Let the people praise thee, O God; let all the people praise thee. Then shall the earth yield her increase; and God, even our own God, shall bless us. God shall bless us; and all the ends of the earth shall [hold him in awe and wonder.]

Quiet

Prayer

Thank you.

Benediction

If the only prayer you said in your whole life was "thank you," that would suffice.

Meister Eckhart[1]

Friday

Evening

Introit

God's mercy is manifest in the number of chances he gives us to get it right.

Gospel

MATTHEW 25:31-45 "When the Son of Man comes in his glory, and all the angels with him, then he will sit on the throne of his glory. All the nations will be gathered before him, and he will separate people one from another as a shepherd separates the sheep from the goats, and he will put the sheep at his right hand and the goats at the left. Then the king will say to those at his right hand, 'Come, you that are blessed by my Father, inherit the kingdom prepared for you from the foundation of the world; for I was hungry and you gave me food, I was thirsty and you gave me something to drink, I was a stranger and you welcomed me, I was naked and you gave me clothing, I was sick and you took care of me, I was in prison and you visited me." Then the righteous will answer him, 'Lord, when was it that we saw you hungry and gave you food, or thirsty and gave you something to drink? And when was it that we saw you a stranger and welcomed you, or naked and gave you clothing? And when was it that we saw you sick or in prison and visited you?' And the king will answer them, 'Truly I tell you, just as you did it to one of the least of these who are members of my family, you did it to me.' Then he will say to those at his left hand… 'I was hungry and you gave me no food, I was thirsty and you gave me nothing to drink, I was a stranger and you did not welcome me, naked and you did not give me clothing, sick and in prison and you did not visit me.' Then they also will answer, 'Lord, when was it that we saw you hungry or thirsty or a stranger or naked or sick or in prison, and did not take care of you?' Then he will answer them, 'Truly I tell you, just as you did not do it to one of the least of these, you did not do it to me.'"

Lord, you have already come and are here among us. Help us to serve you in each other, not to inherit a kingdom in the future, but to help create your kingdom here and now.

Epistle

HEBREWS 13:1-3 Let mutual love continue. Do not neglect to show hospitality to strangers, for by doing that some have entertained angels without knowing it. Remember those who are in prison, as though you were in prison with them; those who are being tortured, as though you yourselves were being tortured.

Psalm

PSALM 119:169-176 Let my cry come near before thee, O LORD: give me understanding according to thy word. Let my supplication come before thee: deliver me according to thy word. My lips shall utter praise, when thou hast taught me thy statutes. My tongue shall speak of thy word: for all thy commandments are righteousness. Let thine hand help me; for I have chosen thy precepts. I have longed for thy salvation, O LORD; and thy law is my delight. Let my soul live, and it shall praise thee; and let thy judgments help me. I have gone astray like a lost sheep; seek thy servant; for I do not forget thy commandments.

Quiet

Prayer

Why are there those who hunger?
Why are there those who thirst?
Why are there those who are strangers?
Why are there those who are naked?
Why are there those who are sick?
Why are there those who are in prison?

Whatever the reasons,
All those are, and more.

Whatever the reasons,
There is also Your gift of compassion.

Help me to share it with all those around me.

Benediction

Serve and listen.

Friday Night

Introit

For what are you trying to hold back time and save the energy of your life? What would be worth your life? What will be worth your life?

Gospel

JOHN 12:24 "Very truly, I tell you, unless a grain of wheat falls into the earth and dies, it remains just a single grain; but if it dies, it bears much fruit.

MARK 8:34-36 He called the crowd with his disciples, and said to them, "If any want to become my followers, let them deny themselves and take up their cross and follow me. For those who want to save their life will lose it, and those who lose their life for my sake, and for the sake of the gospel, will save it. For what will it profit them to gain the whole world and forfeit their life?"

JOHN 12:26-27 "Whoever serves me must follow me, and where I am, there will my servant be also. Whosoever serves me, the

Father will honor. Now my soul is troubled. And what should I say - 'Father, save me from this hour?' No, it is for this reason that I have come to this hour."

Epistle

ROMANS 5:7-8 Indeed, rarely will anyone die for a righteous person - though perhaps for a good person someone might actually dare to die. But God proves his love for us in that while we were still sinners Christ died for us.

And now he asks us to give up our lives for each other, to live and die for each other.

Psalm

PSALM 136:1-9, 26 O give thanks unto the LORD; for he is good: for his mercy endureth forever. O give thanks unto the God of gods: for his mercy endureth for ever. O give thanks to the Lord of lords: for his mercy endureth forever. To him who alone doeth great wonders: for his mercy endureth forever. To him that by wisdom made the heavens: for his mercy endureth for ever. To him that stretched out the earth above the waters: for his mercy endureth forever. To him that made great lights: for his mercy endureth forever: The sun to rule by day: for his mercy endureth forever: The moon and stars to rule by night: for his mercy endureth forever. O give thanks unto the God of heaven: for his mercy endureth forever.

Quiet

Prayer

Lord, why did you tell me to love all men, my brothers?
I have tried but I come back to you, frightened…

Lord, I was so peaceful at home, I was so comfortably settled.
It was well furnished and I felt cozy.
I was alone, I was at peace,
Sheltered from the wind, the rain, the mud.
I would have stayed unsullied in my ivory tower.

But, Lord, you have discovered a breach in my defenses,
you have forced me to open my door,
like a squall of rain in the face, the cry of men has awakened me.
Like a gale of wind a friendship has shaken me,
As a ray of light slips in unnoticed, your grace has stirred me
…and, rashly enough, I left my door ajar. Now, Lord, I am lost!

Outside men were lying in wait for me.
I did not know they were so near; in this house, in this street, in this office; my neighbor, my colleague, my friend.

As soon as I started to open the door I saw them with outstretched hands, burning eyes, longing hearts, like beggars on church steps.

The first ones came in, Lord. There was after all some space in my heart.

I welcomed them. I would have cared for them and fondled them, my very own little lambs, my little flock.

You would have been pleased Lord, I would have served you and honored you in a proper respectable way.

Till then it was sensible…

But the next ones, Lord, the other men, I had not seen them: they were hidden behind the first ones.

There were more of them, they were wretched; they overpowered me without warning.

We had to crowd in, I had to find room for them.

Now they have come from all over, in successive waves, pushing one another, jostling one another.

They have come from all over town, from all parts of the country, of the world; numberless, inexhaustible.

They don't come alone any longer but in groups, bound to one another.

They come bending under heavy loads; loads of injustice, of resentment and hate, of suffering and sin…

They drag the world behind them, with everything rusted, twisted, or badly adjusted.

Lord, they hurt me! They are in the way, they are everywhere.
They are too hungry, they are consuming me!
I can't do anything anymore; as they come in, they push
    the door, and the door opens wider...
Lord! my door is wide open!
I can't stand it anymore! It's too much! It's no kind of life! What
    about my job? my family? my peace? my liberty? and me?
Lord, I have lost everything, I don't belong to myself any longer;
There's no more room for me at home.

Don't worry, God says, you have gained all.
While men came in to you,
I, your Father,
I, your God,
Slipped in among them.

Michel Quoist[2]

Calm down. You will always have to be the one to be responsible and figure out what and how much you will do. Drama will not help. Your commitment to love your neighbor and your relationship with Jesus will. Yes, it will cost you your life. But you do not know what that will look like. Just get out of the boat and keep walking and reaching out to Jesus.

Benediction

JOHN 12:26-27 "Whoever serves me must follow me, and where I am, there will my servant be also. Whosoever serves me, the Father will honor. Now my soul is troubled. And what should I say - 'Father, save me from this hour?' No, it is for this reason that I have come to this hour."

Saturday

Saturday

Morning

Introit

Both the call and the promise of discipleship, to love God and my neighbor, are held in the passion of Jesus.

Gospel

MATTHEW 26:1-28 When Jesus had finished saying all these things, he said to his disciples, "You know that after two days the Passover is coming, and the Son of Man will be handed over to be crucified."

Then the chief priests and the elders of the people gathered in the palace of the high priest, who was called Caiaphas, and they conspired to arrest Jesus by stealth and kill him. But they said, "Not during the festival, or there may be a riot among the people."

Now while Jesus was at Bethany in the house of Simon the leper, a woman came to him with an alabaster jar of very costly ointment, and she poured it on his head as he sat at the table. But when the disciples saw it, they were angry and said, "Why this waste? For this ointment could have been sold for a large sum, and the money given to the poor." But Jesus, aware of this, said to them,

"Why do you trouble the woman? She has performed a good service for me. For you always have the poor with you, but you will not always have me. By pouring this ointment on my body she has prepared me for burial. Truly I tell you, wherever this good news is proclaimed in the whole world, what she has done will be told in remembrance of her."

Then one of the twelve, who was called Judas Iscariot, went to the chief priests and said, "What will you give me if I betray him to you?" They paid him thirty pieces of silver. And from that moment he began to look for an opportunity to betray him.

On the first day of Unleavened Bread the disciples came to Jesus, saying, "Where do you want us to make the preparations for you to eat the Passover?" He said, "Go into the city to a certain man, and say to him, 'The Teacher says, My time is near; I will keep the Passover at your house with my disciples.' " So the disciples did as Jesus had directed them, and they prepared the Passover meal.

When it was evening, he took his place with the twelve; and while they were eating, he said, "Truly I tell you, one of you will betray me." And they became greatly distressed and began to say to him one after another, "Surely not I, Lord?" He answered, "The one who has dipped his hand into the bowl with me will betray me. The Son of Man goes as it is written of him, but woe to that one by whom the Son of Man is betrayed! It would have been better for that one not to have been born." Judas, who betrayed him, said, "Surely not I, Rabbi?" He replied, "You have said so."

While they were eating, Jesus took a loaf of bread, and after blessing it he broke it, gave it to the disciples, and said, "Take, eat; this is my body." Then he took a cup, and after giving thanks he gave it to them, saying, "Drink from it, all of you; for this is my blood of the covenant, which is poured out for many for the forgiveness of sins."

While you have been comforted, whom have you left without comfort? What friend have you betrayed? And what was your thirty pieces of silver?

Epistle

GALATIANS 5:14, 22-23 For the whole law is summed up in a single commandment, "You shall love your neighbor as yourself."

…the fruit of the Spirit is love, joy, peace, patience, kindness, generosity, faithfulness, gentleness, and self-control. There is no law against such things.

GALATIANS 6:1-2, 9-10 My friends, if anyone is detected in a transgression, you who have received the Spirit should restore such a one in a spirit of gentleness. Take care that you yourselves are not tempted. Bear one another's burdens, and in this way you will fulfill the law of Christ. So let us not grow weary of doing what is right, for we will reap at harvest time, if we do not give up. Whenever we have an opportunity, let us work for the good of all…

Psalm

PSALM 130:1-8 Out of the depths have I cried unto thee, O LORD. Lord, hear my voice: let thine ears be attentive to the voice of my supplications. If thou, LORD, shouldest mark iniquities, O Lord, who shall stand? But there is forgiveness with thee… I wait for the LORD, my soul doth wait, and in his word do I hope. My soul waiteth for the Lord more than they that watch for the morning: I say, more than they that watch for the morning. Let Israel hope in the LORD: for with the LORD there is mercy, and with him is plenteous redemption. And he shall redeem Israel from all his iniquities.

Thank you, LORD.

Quiet

Prayer

Our Father who art in Heaven, hallowed be Thy name. Thy Kingdom come. Thy will be done on earth, as it is in Heaven. Give us this day our daily bread. And forgive us our trespasses, as we forgive those who trespass against us. And lead us not into temptation, but deliver us from evil. For Thine is the Kingdom, and the power and the glory for ever and ever. Amen.

Benediction

Wir essen und leben wohl in rechten Osterfladen.
Der alte Sauerteig nicht soll sein bei dem Wort Gnaden.
Christus will die Koste sein
und speisen die Seel allein.
Der Glaub will kein andern leben.
Halleluja!

With loving hearts we keep today the feast God hath us given.
Before his work, in defeat, retreats the ancient leaven.
Christ himself the feast hath spread.
By him the hungry soul is fed,
with living bread come down from heaven.
Alleluia!

Martin Luther[1]

Saturday

Day

Introit

Both the call and the promise of discipleship, to love God and my neighbor, are held in the passion of Jesus.

Gospel

JOHN 13:2-9, 12-15, 34-35 And during supper Jesus, knowing that the Father had given all things into his hands, and that he had come from God and was going to God, got up from the table, took off his outer robe, and tied a towel around himself. Then he poured water into a basin and began to wash the disciples' feet and to wipe them with the towel that was tied around him. He came to Simon Peter, who said to him, "Lord, are you going to wash my feet?" Jesus answered, "You do not know now what I am doing, but later you will understand." Peter said to him, "You will never wash my feet." Jesus answered, "Unless I wash you, you have no share with me." Simon Peter said to him, "Lord, not my feet only but also my hands and my head!"

After he had washed their feet, had put on his robe, and had returned to the table, he said to them, "Do you know what I have done to you? You call me Teacher and Lord - and you are right, for that is what I am. So if I, your Lord and Teacher, have washed your feet, you also ought to wash one another's feet. For I have set you an example, that you also should do as I have done to you.

"I give you a new commandment, that you love one another. Just as I have loved you, you also should love one another. By this everyone will know that you are my disciples, if you have love for one another."

JOHN 15:12-13 "This is my commandment, that you love one another as I have loved you. No one has greater love than this, to lay down one's life for one's friends."

Epistle

I TIMOTHY 4:12 …set the believers an example in speech and conduct, in love, in faith, in purity.

Psalm

PSALM 119: 33-35 Teach me, O LORD, the way of thy statutes; and I shall keep it unto the end. Give me understanding, and I shall keep thy law; yea, I shall observe it with my whole heart. Make me to go in the path of thy commandments; for therein do I delight.

Thank you, LORD.

Quiet

Prayer

Jesus, priceless treasure, source of purest pleasure,
friend most sure and true:
Long my heart was burning, fainting much and yearning,
thirsting after you.
Yours I am, O spotless lamb, I will let nothing hide you,
seek no joy beside you.

Johann Franck[2]

Benediction

JOHN 13:34-35 "I give you a new commandment, that you love one another. Just as I have loved you, you also should love one another. By this everyone will know that you are my disciples, if you have love for one another."

Saturday

Afternoon

Introit

Both the call and the promise of discipleship, to love God and my neighbor, are held in the passion of Jesus.

Gospel

MATTHEW 26:30-53, 55-56 When they had sung the hymn, they went out to the Mount of Olives. Then Jesus said to them, "You will all become deserters because of me this night; for it is written, 'I will strike the shepherd, and the sheep of the flock will be scattered.' But after I am raised up, I will go ahead of you to Galilee." Peter said to him, "Though all become deserters because of you, I will never desert you." Jesus said to him, "Truly I tell you, this very night, before the cock crows, you will deny me three times." Peter said to him, "Even though I must die with you, I will not deny you." And so said all the disciples.

Then Jesus went with them to a place called Gethsemane; and he said to his disciples, "Sit here while I go over there and pray." He took with him Peter and the two sons of Zebedee, and began to be grieved and agitated. Then he said to them, "I am deeply grieved, even to death; remain here, and stay awake with me." And going a little farther, he threw himself on the ground and prayed, "My Father, if it is possible, let this cup pass from me; yet not what I want but what you want." Then he came to the disciples and found them sleeping; and he said to Peter, "So, could you not stay awake with me one hour? Stay awake and pray that you may not come into the time of trial; the spirit indeed is willing, but the flesh is weak." Again he went away for the second time and prayed, "My Father, if this cannot pass unless I drink it, your will be done." Again he came and found them sleeping, for their eyes were heavy. So leaving them again, he went away and prayed for the third time, saying the same words. Then he came to the disciples and said to them, "Are you still sleeping and taking your rest? See, the hour is at hand, and the Son of Man is betrayed into the hands of sinners. Get up, let us be going. See, my betrayer is at hand."

While he was still speaking, Judas, one of the twelve, arrived; with him was a large crowd with swords and clubs, from the chief priests and the elders of the people. Now the betrayer had given them a sign, saying, "The one I will kiss is the man; arrest him." At once he came up to Jesus and said, "Greetings, Rabbi!" and kissed him. Jesus said to him, "Friend, do what you are here to do." Then they came and laid hands on Jesus and arrested him. Suddenly, one of those with Jesus put his hand on his sword, drew it, and struck the slave of the high priest, cutting off his ear. Then Jesus said to him, "Put your sword back into its place; for all who take the sword will perish by the sword. Do you think that I cannot appeal to my Father, and he will at once send me more than twelve legions of angels?" At that hour Jesus said to the crowds,

"Have you come out with swords and clubs to arrest me as though I were a bandit? Day after day I sat in the temple teaching, and you did not arrest me."

…Then all the disciples deserted him and fled.

Epistle

I PETER 3:8-19 Finally, all of you, have unity of spirit, sympathy, love for one another, a tender heart, and a humble mind. Do not repay evil for evil or abuse for abuse; but, on the contrary, repay with a blessing. It is for this that you were called - that you might inherit a blessing. For "Those who desire life and desire to see good days, let them keep their tongues from evil and their lips from speaking deceit; let them turn away from evil and do good; let them seek peace and pursue it. For the eyes of the Lord are on the righteous, and his ears are open to their prayer. But the face of the Lord is against those who do evil." Now who will it harm if you are eager to do what is good? But even if you do suffer for doing what is right, you are blessed. Do not fear what they fear, and do not be intimidated, but in your hearts sanctify Christ as Lord. Always be ready to make your defense to anyone who demands from you an accounting for the hope that is in you; yet do it with gentleness and reverence. Keep your conscience clear, so that, when you are maligned, those who abuse you for your good conduct in Christ may be put to shame. For it is better to suffer for doing good, if suffering should be God's will, than to suffer for doing evil. For Christ also suffered for sins once for all, the righteous for the unrighteous, in order to bring you to God. He was put to death in the flesh, but made alive in the spirit…

Psalm

PSALM 55:1-8, 12-14, 16-18, 22 Give ear to my prayer, O God; and hide not thyself from my supplication. Attend unto me, and hear me: I mourn in my complaint, and make a noise; Because of the voice of the enemy, because of the oppression of the wicked: for they cast iniquity upon me, and in wrath they hate me. My heart is sore pained within me: and the terrors of death are fallen upon me. Fearfulness and trembling are come upon me, and horror hath overwhelmed me. And I said, Oh that I had wings like a dove! for then would I fly away, and be at rest. Lo, then would I wander far off, and remain in the wilderness. Selah. I would hasten my escape from the windy storm and tempest. For it was not an enemy that reproached me; then I could have borne it: neither was it he that hated me that did magnify himself against me; then I would have hid myself from him: But it was thou, a man mine equal, my guide, and mine acquaintance. We took sweet counsel together, and walked unto the house of God in company.

As for me, I will call upon God; and the LORD shall save me. Evening, and morning, and at noon, will I pray, and cry aloud: and he shall hear my voice. He hath delivered my soul in peace from the battle that was against me: for there were many against me.

Cast thy burden upon the LORD, and he shall sustain thee: he shall never suffer the righteous to be moved...

Thank you, LORD.

Quiet

Prayer

Agnus Dei, qui tollis peccata mundi, miserere nobis.

Agnus Dei, qui tollis peccata mundi, miserere nobis.

Agnus Dei, qui tollis peccata mundi, dona nobis pacem.

Lamb of God, that taketh away the sins of the world, have mercy upon us.

Lamb of God, that taketh away the sins of the world, have mercy upon us.

Lamb of God, that taketh away the sins of the world, grant us peace.

Benediction

I PETER 1:22 Now that you have purified your souls by your obedience to the truth so that you have genuine mutual love, love one another deeply from the heart.

I PETER 4:8 Above all, maintain constant love for one another, for love covers a multitude of sins.

Saturday

Evening

Introit

Both the call and the promise of discipleship, to love God and my neighbor, are held in the passion of Jesus.

Gospel

MATTHEW 26:57-75 Those who had arrested Jesus took him to Caiaphas the high priest, in whose house the scribes and the elders had gathered. But Peter was following him at a distance, as far as the courtyard of the high priest; and going inside, he sat with the guards in order to see how this would end. Now the chief priests and the whole council were looking for false testimony against Jesus so that they might put him to death, but they found none, though many false witnesses came forward. At last two came forward and said, "This fellow said, 'I am able to destroy the temple of God and to build it in three days.'" The high priest stood up and said, "Have you no answer? What is it that they testify against you?" But Jesus was silent. Then the high priest said to him, "I put you under oath before the living God, tell us if you are the Messiah, the Son of God." Jesus said to him, "You have said so..." Then the high priest tore his clothes and said, "He has blasphemed! Why do we still need witnesses? You have now heard his blasphemy. What is your verdict?" They answered, "He deserves death." Then they spat in his face and struck him; and some slapped him, saying, "Prophesy to us, you Messiah! Who is it that struck you?"

Now Peter was sitting outside in the courtyard. A servant-girl came to him and said, "You also were with Jesus the Galilean." But he denied it before all of them, saying, "I do not know what you are talking about." When he went out to the porch, another servant-girl saw him, and she said to the bystanders, "This man was with Jesus of Nazareth." Again he denied it with an oath, "I do not know the man." After a little while the bystanders came up and said to Peter, "Certainly you are also one of them, for your accent betrays you." Then he began to curse, and he swore an oath, "I do not know the man!" At that moment the cock crowed. Then Peter remembered what Jesus had said: "Before the cock crows, you will deny me three times." And he went out and wept bitterly.

MATTHEW 27:1-8, 11-18, 20-44 When morning came, all the chief priests and the elders of the people conferred together against Jesus in order to bring about his death. They bound him, led him away, and handed him over to Pilate the governor.

When Judas, his betrayer, saw that Jesus was condemned, he repented and brought back the thirty pieces of silver to the chief priests and the elders. He said, "I have sinned by betraying innocent blood." But they said, "What is that to us? See to it yourself." Throwing down the pieces of silver in the temple, he departed; and he went and hanged himself. But the chief priests, taking the pieces of silver, said, "It is not lawful to put them into the treasury, since they are blood money." After conferring together, they used them to buy the potter's field as a place to bury foreigners. For this reason that field has been called the Field of Blood to this day.

Consider that God had forgiven Judas and that the problem was that Judas had not forgiven himself. So it may be with us.

Now Jesus stood before the governor; and the governor asked him, "Are you the King of the Jews?" Jesus said, "You say so." But when he was accused by the chief priests and elders, he did not answer. Then Pilate said to him, "Do you not hear how many accusations they make against you?" But he gave him no answer, not even to a single charge, so that the governor was greatly amazed.

Now at the festival the governor was accustomed to release a prisoner for the crowd, anyone whom they wanted. At that time they had a notorious prisoner, called Jesus Barabbas. So after they had gathered, Pilate said to them, "Whom do you want me to release for you, Jesus Barabbas or Jesus who is called the Messiah?" For he realized that it was out of jealousy that they had handed him over. Now the chief priests and the elders persuaded the crowds to ask for Barabbas and to have Jesus killed. The governor again said to them, "Which of the two do you want me to release for you?" And they said, "Barabbas." Pilate said to them, "Then what should I do with Jesus who is called the Messiah?" All of them said, "Let him be crucified!" Then he asked, "Why, what evil has he done?" But they shouted all the more, "Let him be crucified!"

So when Pilate saw that he could do nothing, but rather that a riot was beginning, he took some water and washed his hands before the crowd, saying, "I am innocent of this man's blood; see to it yourselves." Then the people as a whole answered, "His blood be on us and on our children!" So he released Barabbas for them; and after flogging Jesus, he handed him over to be crucified.

Then the soldiers of the governor took Jesus into the governor's headquarters, and they gathered the whole cohort around him. They stripped him and put a scarlet robe on him, and after twisting some thorns into a crown, they put it on his head. They put a reed in his right hand and knelt before him and mocked him, saying, "Hail, King of the Jews!" They spat on him, and took the reed and struck him on the head. After mocking him, they stripped him of the robe and put his own clothes on him. Then they led him away to crucify him.

As they went out, they came upon a man from Cyrene named Simon; they compelled this man to carry his cross. And when they came to a place called Golgotha (which means Place of a Skull), they offered him wine to drink, mixed with gall; but when he tasted it, he would not drink it. And when they had crucified him, they divided his clothes among themselves by casting lots; then they sat down there and kept watch over him. Over his head they put the charge against him, which read, "This is Jesus, the King of the Jews." Then two bandits were crucified with him, one on his right and one on his left. Those who passed by derided him, shaking their heads and saying, "You who would destroy the temple and build it in three days, save yourself! If you are the Son of God, come down from the cross." In the same way the chief priests also, along with the scribes and elders, were mocking him, saying, "He saved others; he cannot save himself. He is the King of Israel; let him come down from the cross now, and we will believe in him. He trusts in God; let God deliver him now, if he wants to; for he said, 'I am God's Son.' " The bandits who were crucified with him also taunted him in the same way.

LUKE 23:34 Then Jesus said, "Father, forgive them; for they do not know what they are doing."

𝓜artin Luther King, Jr., believed that this was Jesus' finest hour, this response of unconditional love, of forgiveness, in the face of such hatred, this demonstration of overcoming evil with good.[3]

Forgiveness is an extraordinary expression of love that allows for all other expressions of love. Consider that unless we forgive we cannot love. And forgive not just once, but again and again, as often as it is called for. And no retaliation against those who injure us or wish to. Never. Everything we do must be done to reach out and help our enemies recover their capacity to be forgiven, to forgive, and to love.

If we retaliate, there is likelihood of future retaliation. If we forgive, there is the possibility of future forgiveness.

To forgive is to give the gift of freedom to oneself and to the one who is forgiven; the freedom from having to repeat the past and the freedom for a new present and a new future.

Consider that if I forgive you, I choose to break the cycle of "an eye for an eye." You have taken my eye and I will not take yours. Not even if you take my other eye. Not now. Not ever. Everything done in retaliation will doom us to a present and future like the past. I trust that everything done in love will give us the opportunity to work together to create a new present and a new future.

MATTHEW 27:46-50, 55-61 And about three o'clock Jesus cried with a loud voice, "Eli, Eli, lema sabachthani?" that is, "My God, my God, why have you forsaken me?" When some of the bystanders heard it, they said, "This man is calling for Elijah." At once one of them ran and got a sponge, filled it with sour wine, put it on a stick, and gave it to him to drink. But the others said, "Wait, let us see whether Elijah will come to save him." Then Jesus cried again with a loud voice and breathed his last.

Many women were also there, looking on from a distance; they had followed Jesus from Galilee and had provided for him. Among them were Mary Magdalene, and Mary the mother of James and Joseph, and the mother of the sons of Zebedee.

When it was evening, there came a rich man from Arimathea, named Joseph, who was also a disciple of Jesus. He went to Pilate and asked for the body of Jesus; then Pilate ordered it to be given to him. So Joseph took the body and wrapped it in a clean linen cloth and laid it in his own new tomb, which he had hewn in the rock. He then rolled a great stone to the door of the tomb and went away. Mary Magdalene and the other Mary were there, sitting opposite the tomb.

Epistle

I PETER 2:1, 12, 21-23 Rid yourselves, therefore, of all malice, and all guile, insincerity, envy, and all slander. Conduct yourselves honorably among the Gentiles, so that, though they malign you as evildoers, they may see your honorable deeds and glorify God when he comes to judge. For to this you have been called, because Christ also suffered for you, leaving you an example, so that you should follow in his steps. "He committed no sin, and no deceit was found in his mouth." When he was abused, he did not return abuse; when he suffered, he did not threaten; but he entrusted himself to the one who judges justly.

Psalm

PSALM 107:1, 8-9 O give thanks unto the LORD, for he is good: for his mercy endureth forever. Oh that men would praise the LORD for his goodness, and for his wonderful works to the children of men! For he satisfieth the longing soul, and filleth the hungry soul with goodness.

Thank you, LORD.

Quiet

Prayer

Amazing grace, how sweet the sound,
that saved a wretch like me!
I once was lost, but now am found,
was blind but now I see.

John Newton[4]

Benediction

What wondrous love is this, O my soul, O my soul,
What wondrous love is this, O my soul!
What wondrous love is this that caused the Lord of bliss
To bear the dreadful curse for my soul, for my soul,
To bear the dreadful curse for my soul!

American Folk Hymn[5]

Saturday

Night

Introit

Both the call and the promise of discipleship, to love God and my neighbor, are held in the passion of Jesus. So ask yourself again, what will you give in gratitude for the life you have been given?

Gospel

JOHN 21:1-13, 15-17 [After his resurrection] Jesus showed himself again to the disciples by the Sea of Tiberias; and he showed himself in this way. Gathered there together were Simon Peter, Thomas called the Twin, Nathanael of Cana in Galilee, the sons of Zebedee, and two others of his disciples. Simon Peter said to them, "I am going fishing." They said to him, "We will go with you." They went out and got into the boat, but that night they caught nothing.

Just after daybreak, Jesus stood on the beach; but the disciples did not know that it was Jesus. Jesus said to them, "Children, you have no fish, have you?" They answered him, "No." He said to them, "Cast the net to the right side of the boat, and you will find some."

So they cast it, and now they were not able to haul it in because there were so many fish. That disciple whom Jesus loved said to Peter, "It is the Lord!" When Simon Peter heard that it was the Lord, he put on some clothes, for he was naked, and jumped into the sea. But the other disciples came in the boat, dragging the net full of fish, for they were not far from the land, only about a hundred yards off.

When they had gone ashore, they saw a charcoal fire there, with fish on it, and bread. Jesus said to them, "Bring some of the fish that you have just caught." So Simon Peter went aboard and hauled the net ashore, full of large fish, a hundred fifty-three of them; and though there were so many, the net was not torn. Jesus said to them, "Come and have breakfast." Now none of the disciples dared to ask him, "Who are you?" because they knew it was the Lord. Jesus came and took the bread and gave it to them, and did the same with the fish.

When they had finished breakfast, Jesus said to Simon Peter, "Simon son of John, do you love me?" He said to him, "Yes, Lord; you know that I love you." Jesus said to him, "Feed my lambs." A second time he said to him, "Simon son of John, do you love me?" He said to him, "Yes, Lord; you know that I love you." Jesus said to him, "Tend my sheep." He said to him the third time, "Simon son of John, do you love me?" Peter felt hurt because he said to him the third time, "Do you love me?" And he said to him, "Lord, you know everything; you know that I love you." Jesus said to him, "Feed my sheep."

All is forgiven. "Feed my sheep."

Epistle

I JOHN 3:11, 16-18 For this is the message you have heard from the beginning, that we should love one another. We know love by this, that he laid down his life for us - and we ought to lay down our lives for one another. How does God's love abide in anyone who has the world's goods and sees a brother or sister in need and yet refuses help? Little children, let us love, not in word or speech, but in truth and action.

I JOHN 4:16 So we have known and believe the love that God has for us. God is love, and those who abide in love abide in God, and God abides in them.

II JOHN 1:5-6 …I ask you, not as though I were writing you a new commandment, but one we have had from the beginning, let us love one another. And this is love, that we walk according to his commandments; this is the commandment just as you have heard it from the beginning - you must walk in it.

Psalm

PSALM 100:1-5 Make a joyful noise unto the LORD, all ye lands. Serve the LORD with gladness: come before his presence with singing. Know ye that the LORD he is God: it is he that hath made us, and not we ourselves; we are his people, and the sheep of his pasture. Enter into his gates with thanksgiving, and into his courts with praise: be thankful unto him, and bless his name. For the LORD is good; his mercy is everlasting; and his truth endureth to all generations.

Thank you, LORD.

Quiet

Prayer

O Lord, thank you for a heart that I can pour out in compassion. Thank you for a life that I can spend in thy service. Amen.

Benediction

JOHN 21:17 He said to him the third time, "Simon son of John, do you love me?" Peter felt hurt because he said to him the third time, "Do you love me?" And he said to him, "Lord, you know everything; you know that I love you." Jesus said to him, "Feed my sheep."

ACTS 1:11 "… Men of Galilee, why do you stand looking up toward heaven?"

MATTHEW 28:20 "And remember, I am with you always, to the end of the age."

Notes

Foreword

(1) Quoted in "What are current Living School students experiencing? A Conversation with Peter Mathies," by Peter Mathies, in *The Mendicant,* Vol. IV, No. 3 (May, 2014) Pg. 4.

(2) Merton, Thomas, *A Book of Hours,* edited by Kathleen Deignan. Sorin Books, 2007.

(3) Rauschenbusch, Walter, "The Little Gate to God." Source: *Reformed Christianity,* "The Little Gate to God" (Accessed June 3, 2014). http://www.reformedchristianity.org/poems/god-in-the-experience-of-men/58-the-fellowship-of-god-and-man/283-the-little-gate-to-god.html

(4) Armstrong, Karen, *Twelve Steps to a Compassionate Life.* Alfred A. Knopf, 2010.

(5) http://www.copa-iaf.org

(6) After PHILIPPIANS 4:7 And the peace of God, which passeth all understanding, shall keep your hearts and minds through Jesus Christ. KJV

Introduction

(1) *A Book of Hours.* Pg. 15.

(2) Chesterton, G. K., *What's Wrong With the World.* Empire Books, 2011. Pg. 22. Originally published in 1910. The actual quote reads,

"Men have not got tired of Christianity; they have never found enough Christianity to get tired of."

(3) *A Book of Hours.* Pp. 9-12, 15-42.

(4) *Twelve Steps to a Compassionate Life.*

(5) Schweitzer, Albert, *Out of My Life and Thought*, translated by Antje Bultmann Lemke. The Johns Hopkins University Press, 2009. Originally published by Henry Holt and Company, Inc., 1933, 1949.

(6) Gandhi, Mahatma, *The Essential Gandhi, An Anthology of His Writings on His Life, Work, and Ideas*, edited by Louis Fischer. Vintage Books, 1962.

(7) King, Martin Luther, Jr., A *Testament of Hope, The Essential Writings and Speeches of Martin Luther King, Jr.*, edited by James M. Washington. HarperCollins Publishers, 1986.

(8) Yoder, John Howard, *The Politics of Jesus.* William B. Eerdmans Publishing Company, 1972.

(9) *A Book of Hours.* Pg. 10.

(10) *A Book of Hours.* Pp. 21-24.

(11) Armstrong, Karen, *The Bible, a Biography.* Grove Press, 2007. Pp. 126-154.

(12) Finley, James, *The Contemplative Heart.* Sorin Books, 2000. Pg. 46.

(13) *A Book of Hours.* Pg. 23.

(14) *A Book of Hours.* Pg. 209.

Sunday

(1) Godwin, Gail, "Genealogy and Grace," in *Watch for the Light, Readings for Advent and Christmas*. The Plough Publishing House, 2001. Pp. 159-167.

(2) Mahatma Gandhi might have said, "We need to be the change we wish to see in the world." However, this was actually said by his grandson, Arun Gandhi, in speaking about his grandfather's life and work, in the newspaper article, "Arun Gandhi Shares the Mahatma's Message," by Michel W. Potts, in *India–West* [San Leandro, California], Vol. XXVII, No. 13 (1 February, 2002) Pg. A34.

(3) Schweitzer, Albert, *Reverence for Life*, translated by Reginald H. Fuller. Harper and Row, 1969. Pg. 54.

(4) Gahan, William, "The Christian's Guide to Heaven, 1794," in *The Oxford Book of Prayer*, edited by George Appleton. Oxford University Press, 1985. Pg. 133.

(5) Runcie, Robert, *The Oxford Book of Prayer*. Pg. 123.

(6) Le Guin, Ursula K., *The Left Hand of Darkness*. Ace Books, 1969. Pg. 246.

Monday

(1) Rumi, Mevlana. Source: *Quotes by Mevlana Rumi. A Mevlana Rumi Quote Library/The Gaiam Blog* (Accessed August 28, 2014). http://blog.gaiam.com/quotes/authors/mevlana-rumi?page=16

(2) Cotter, Jim, *Prayer at Night - A Book for the Darkness*. Cairns Publications, 1991. Pg. 42.

(3) Niebuhr, Reinhold, *The Oxford Book of Prayer*. Pg. 71.

(4) Wesley, John, *The Oxford Book of Prayer*. Pg. 73.

Tuesday

(1) *Prayers of the Cosmos*, edited and translated by Neil Douglas-Klotz. HarperCollins Publishers, 1994. Pg. 41.

(2) Old Sarum Primer, *The Oxford Book of Prayer*. Pg. 90.

Wednesday

(1) Schweitzer's sermon, "The Life of Service," in *Reverence for Life*. Pp. 58-66.

(2) Dorsey, Thomas, *The Notre Dame Book of Prayer*, edited by Heidi Schlumpf. Ave Maria Press, 2010. Pg. 257.

(3) St. Francis of Assisi, *The Oxford Book of Prayer*. Pg. 75. Although attributed to St. Francis of Assisi, the prayer seems to have first appeared in 1912, in a small devotional magazine, *La Clochette*, published by La Ligue de la Sainte-Messe, founded by Fr. Esther Bouquerel. The author was not named, but may have been Fr. Bouquerel. The first known English translation appeared in the Quaker magazine, *Friends' Intelligencer*, in 1927. Source: *Wikipedia*, "Prayer of St. Francis" (Accessed March 11, 2014). http://en.wikipedia.org/wiki/Prayer_of_St._Francis

Thursday

(1) Tukaram, *An Indian Peasant Mystic*, edited and translated by John S. Hoyland. H. R. Allenson, Ltd., 1932. Pg. 67.

(2) St. Augustine, *The Notre Dame Book of Prayer*. Pp. 90-91.

(3) Jowett, J. H., *The Oxford Book of Prayer*. Pg. 92.

(4) JEREMIAH 31:34 No longer shall they teach one another, or say to each other, "Know the LORD," for they shall all know me, from the least of them to the greatest, says the LORD; for I will forgive their iniquity, and remember their sin no more. *NRSV*

(5) Prayer written by an unknown prisoner in Ravensbrück concentration camp and left by the body of a dead child, in *Blessings*, by Mary Craig. Sorin Books, 2000. Pg. 132.

Friday

(1) Meister Eckhart, *The Notre Dame Book of Prayer*. Pg. 145.

(2) Quoist, Michel, *The Oxford Book of Prayer*. Pp. 76-77. Orig. published in *Prayers of Life*, by Michel Quoist. Gill and Macmillan, 1965.

Saturday

(1) Luther, Martin, "Wir essen und leben wohl," chorale from *Christ lag in Todesbanden*, Cantata BWV 4, by Johann Sebastian Bach.

(2) Franck, Johann, "Jesus, Priceless Treasure," translated by Catherine Winkworth, Hymn #480, in *The New Century Hymnal*. The Pilgrim Press, 1995.

(3) King, Martin Luther, Jr., "Love in Action," in *Strength to Love*. Fortress Press, 2010. Pp. 31-41.

(4) Newton, John, "Amazing Grace," Hymn #547, in *The New Century Hymnal*. The Pilgrim Press, 1995.

(5) American folk hymn, "What Wondrous Love Is This," Hymn #432, in *The Methodist Hymnal*. The Methodist Publishing House, 1966.

Additional Suggested Reading

Campbell, Don, *Music, Physician for Times to Come*. Quest Books, The Theosophical Publishing House, 1991. An anthology exploring the relationship between music and well-being.

Kornfield, Jack, *The Art of Forgiveness, Lovingkindness, and Peace*. Bantam Books, 2002. Guided meditations for compassionate living.

Thich Nhat Hanh, *Living Buddha, Living Christ*. Penguin Group, 1995. The common path of these two lives of compassion and holiness.

Wattles, Jeffrey, *The Golden Rule*. Oxford University Press, 1996. An historical survey of the golden rule in philosophy, ethics, psychology, and religion and concluding with a synthesis of these interpretations in an ethics of relationship.

Discography

The Benedictine Monks of Santo Domingo De Silos, *Gregorian Chant: The Definitive Collection*. Milan Entertainment, Inc., 2008.

Chanticleer, *Mysteria, Gregorian Chants*. Teldec, 1995.

The Tallis Scholars, *Sarum Chant, Missa in Gallicantu*. Gimell Records Ltd., 1988.

Acknowledgements

The author and publisher gratefully acknowledge all the sources from which excerpts were taken. We regret any errors and oversights. Please bring them to our attention and we will correct them in future editions.

Excerpted from *The Oxford Book of Prayer*, edited by George Appleton. Oxford University Press, 1985.

Excerpted from *What's Wrong With the World*, by G. K. Chesterton. Empire Books, 2011. Originally published in 1910. Public domain.

Excerpted from *Prayer at Night*, by Jim Cotter. Cairns Publications, 1991. ISBN 1-870652-01-0. Copyright © 1991 by Jim Cotter. Used with permission of the author.

Excerpted from *Blessings*, by Mary Craig. Sorin Books, 2000.

"The Lord's Prayer (One Possible New Translation from the Aramaic)" [18l.] from *Prayers of the Cosmos: Meditations on the Aramaic Words of Jesus*, by Neil Douglas-Klotz. Copyright © 1990 by Neil Douglas-Klotz. Foreword © 1990 by Matthew Fox. Reprinted by permission of HarperCollins Publishers.

Excerpted from *The Contemplative Heart*, by James Finley. Copyright © 2000 by Ave Maria Press®, Inc., P.O. Box 428, Notre Dame, IN 46556. www.avemariapress.com Used with permission of the publisher.

Excerpted from *The Left Hand of Darkness*, by Ursula K. Le Guin. Copyright © 1969 by Ace Books. Used with permission of the publisher.

Excerpted from "What are current Living School students experiencing? A Conversation with Peter Mathies," by Peter Mathies, in *The Mendicant* Vol. IV, No. 3 (May, 2014) Pg. 4. Copyright © Center for Action and Contemplation. Used with permission of the publisher.

Excerpted from *A Book of Hours*, by Thomas Merton. Copyright © 2007 by Ave Maria Press®, Inc., P.O. Box 428, Notre Dame, IN 46556. www.avemariapress.com Used with permission of the publisher.

Excerpted from *The Methodist Hymnal*. The Methodist Publishing House, 1966. Public domain.

Excerpted from *The New Century Hymnal*. The Pilgrim Press, 1995. Public domain.

Excerpted from *Hymns of Worship*, by Reinhold Niebuhr, edited by Ursula Niebuhr. Copyright © 1939 by Association Press, New York.

Excerpted from the newspaper article, "Arun Gandhi Shares the Mahatma's Message," by Michel W. Potts, in *India-West* [San Leandro, California], Vol. XXVII, No. 13 (1 February 2002).

Excerpted from Walter Rauschenbusch, "The Little Gate to God." Source: *Reformed Christianity*, "The Little Gate to God." (Accessed June 3, 2014). Public domain. http://www.reformedchristianity.org/poems/god-in-the-experience-of-men/58-the-fellowship-of-god-and-man/283-the-little-gate-to-god.html

Excerpted from *Mevlana Rumi. Source: Quotes by Mevlana Rumi. A Mevlana Rumi Quote Library/The Gaiam Blog* (Accessed August 28, 2014). Public domain. http://blog.gaiam.com/quotes/authors/mevlana-rumi?page=16

Excerpted from *The Notre Dame Book of Prayer*, edited by Heidi Schlumpf. Copyright © 2010 by Ave Maria Press®, Inc., P.O. Box 428, Notre Dame, IN 46556. www.avemariapress.com Used with permission of the publisher.

Brief quote from pg. 54 from *Reverence for Life*, by Albert Schweitzer and translated by Reginald H. Fuller. Copyright © 1969 by Rhena Eckert-Schweitzer. Reprinted by permission of HarperCollins Publishers.

Excerpted from *An Indian Peasant Mystic*, by Tukaram, edited and translated by John S. Hoyland. H. R. Allenson Ltd., London, 1932.

About the Author

Art Schuller graduated from North Park University with a major in philosophy. While he intended to become a pastor, he decided instead to practice medicine. He received his MD degree from the University of Illinois, College of Medicine, and continued with specialty training in internal medicine and psychiatry. He taught at the University of Illinois College of Medicine, and the University of California, Davis, School of Medicine. For most of his practice he took care of patients with chronic pain. When he retired he became a hospice volunteer, an advocate for affordable health care for low income and undocumented individuals, and began to serve on community bioethics committees in the Monterey, California area.

Art and his wife, Sandy, and their daughter, Stephanie, live in Carmel Valley, California, where they sing in church and community choirs with great people, ride their Harley-Davidson, try to do good work, and where their dog, Snuffy, thus far has continued to allow them to do her bidding.

All the proceeds from the sale of this book will be contributed to UNICEF, in support of their work improving the lives of children around the world.
www.unicef.org

Carmel, California
www.luckyvalleypress.com

Body Text: Minion 10.5/13.5

Display Text: Copperplate, Diskus,
and Duc de Berry

Wood products used in the manufacture of this book meet the
Sustainable Forestry Initiative® Chain-of-Custody Standards.
www.sfiprogram.org

www.ingramcontent.com/pod-product-compliance
Lightning Source LLC
Chambersburg PA
CBHW050636300426
44112CB00012B/1823